MOMMY MAGIC

450 Ways to Nurture Your Child

Adria Manary

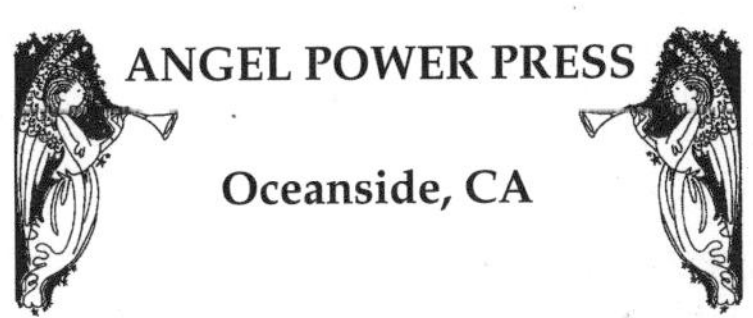
ANGEL POWER PRESS

Oceanside, CA

Cover design by Daria Smith

ISBN: 0-9665830-2-7

Library of Congress Number: 99-096512

Purchase and use of this book constitutes acceptance of the following conditions: that all activities herein contained are to be conducted with appropriate adult supervision; that due care will be exercised by parents or guardians in selection of activities, especially with regard to the age-appropriateness of the activity or suggestion; and that the publisher and/or author shall be in no way liable for any adverse actions or mishaps arising directly or indirectly from any suggestions included in any part of this book.

This book is available at quantity discounts for bulk purchases. For information call 760-721-6666.

Published by:

ANGEL POWER PRESS
P.O. Box 3327
Oceanside, CA 92051
PH: 760-721-6666
FAX: 760-721-6699

I dedicate this book to my precious children,
Chase, Dane and Astra.

My Children Three

My children three
How you please me
Your laughter and your love —
Brighten my days
And soothe my nights
Heartfelt thanks to the Lord above.

Nothing compares
To the love we share
On that we can always depend.
What a gift to me
My children three
Special love that shall never end.

Other Books by Adria Manary

Kennedys — The Next Generation

AND

Touched by a Rainbow

Contact the Author, Send Us Your Stories or Share Your Comments by Visiting Our Fun and Informative Web Site at:

www.mommymagic.com

We Look Forward to Hearing from You!

Table of Contents

PREFACE

When a child is born, God sprinkles a bit of magic into the heart of the mother. Then as the child is laid upon the mother's breast, that magic brings feelings of unparalleled love and incredible awe. From that very moment on, the mother and child reconnect as if the baby were still in the womb. What has been a physical connection for nine months, magically turns into a mental connection that lasts forever.

As life unfolds, the magic that the mother bestows upon her child becomes a springboard for achievement and a safety net for failure. A treasure trove of hope, and the backbone of self-confidence. A blanket to warm the soul and a spark to ignite the spirit.

Outside of the ice rink where my son plays hockey is a sculpture of a mother applauding. The earrings that she is wearing are little ice skates and she has a warm and prideful smile on her face. The quote written beside the statue reads,

"A mother's cheers...
the driving force behind our achievements."

I think that says it all, as long as we remember that our children's achievements in life will not only include winning a championship game or success in their careers – but also the love of family and friends, the respect of their peers, and peace and harmony in their homes.

Instilled deeply inside of a mother's soul is the desire to create a perfect world for her child. However, as the world becomes more and more demanding, we sometimes let the weight of those pressures erode some of the magic that we were blessed with.

It is my hope that this book will help you to keep the magic alive in the midst of the chaotic life that often holds us prisoner. Use it as an occasional reminder — or an "idea a day" guide, to create a strong foundation that the difficulties of life cannot erode. With poems to stir your soul, stories to warm your heart and hundreds of ideas to keep your children smiling — it was written to provide a helpful reference as you strive to create a more enchanting world for your family.

Every child is born with a loving and joyful soul. It is up to us to nurture it and protect it so that it may blossom and leave flowers along the path of their lifetime.

The Magic of a Mother's Love

The magic of a mother's love
Brings harmony and bliss.
It covers like a blanket
And cures boo-boos with a kiss.

It offers grand protection
From evil that lurks 'round,
It tames the fears of little ones
And turns frowns upside down.

It holds a wealth of wisdom
With gentleness it guides,
It holds the hand when needed
Then lets go with tears of pride.

And though those precious childhood years
In an instant pass,
The love and magic she instills
Will last...and last...and last.

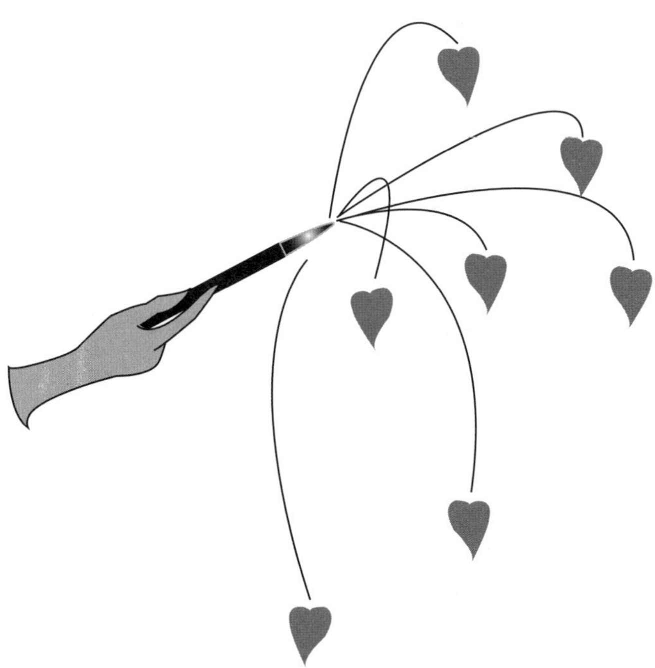

INTRODUCTION: WHAT IS THE "MAGIC?"

It was one of those landmark days when nothing could go wrong. The day began with our regular "morning hugs," my boys got into the bathtub without whining, there were no spills at breakfast, my little girl and I played diving Barbie in the tub for an hour and I still got everything done that I wanted to get done, while my older ones were at school. As a bonus, when I picked them up...they were full of stories to tell without my usual prodding...and they had NO HOMEWORK!

On the way home we stopped at the grocery store and they all rode in one of those new carts with the two red seats in the front, along with the normal front seat inside of the cart. I love those because all three of them have their own special seat. In addition, I could let them get most of the things that they wanted since they were reasonable requests, which made for a great shopping day!

Since they were so good in the store, their reward was to stop for ice cream. I enjoyed a hot fudge sundae as they laughed and gobbled down their own interesting concoctions. I'll never understand how you get bubble gum into ice cream and why you're allowed to swallow it, but my youngest thought it was great. The boys' combinations were too strange to describe. Of course, these are the same boys who mix every kind of soft drink into one cup when they are allowed to get their own at a "make it yourself" soda fountain. We stole each other's cherries and tasted each other's specialties and got spots on our clothes...including mine. But that was part of the fun.

The day got better as we hit the park and finally arrived home to find daddy already in the living room — an unexpected grand finale to an already perfect day. The evening was warmed by loving hearts and a tearjerker movie, topped off by a glowing fire. Some "magic dust" made the fire even more engaging as we tossed it into the flames, which turned into every color of the rainbow. One by one, they all seemed to be drifting off into dreamland...including my husband.

As I stroked their hair, I talked about what a wonderful day we'd had. My six-year-old snuggled up as close as he could possibly get and said, "It was because of the magic, mommy." "What kind of magic are you talking about sweetheart?" I asked. "The magic that's called MOMMY!" he said. The words stood still in my heart as his eyes gazed into mine. Any of Warhol's "fifteen minutes of fame" could never have compared with this. Tears welled up in my eyes and I couldn't respond, so he continued, "YOU make things magic for us, mommy. And I like it."

I realized at that moment, that the magic he was referring to was the everyday environment that a mother is responsible for creating around her child. My mother used to tell me that she wished she could put me in a magic bubble that would protect me from the hurts of the outside world. I have often felt the same way about my own children — but realize that the key is to prepare them to deal with the many disappointments that life will bring, as well as teach them to enjoy every miracle of life, and every precious moment that we have here. This starts early, as they watch how you deal with the roller coaster of life. As you show the way by example, and teach them to uphold the precious virtues of life, you are indeed creating an invisible bubble that will surround their heart and soul, and give them the tools that they will need to become happy, productive and caring adults.

God's words, "...And the greatest of these is love," resonate in my heart constantly. And showing unconditional love to our children is the greatest gift that we can give as parents. Demonstrating that love must be constant and varied, playful and soulful, firm when necessary, kind continually and patient...always.

The following chapters will offer stories, suggestions, tips and activities that will help you on your ceaseless quest to make the world a brighter place for your child. Some of the ideas will awaken the child within you; some you will have heard a million times, yet reading them again will prompt you to try them; some you will never have the desire to try; some you will have done, but the words will remind you how fun it was and you'll want to do it again; some you will have never heard of and you'll say to yourself, "Why didn't I think of that!"; some will bring tears to your eyes, as you remember your mom doing the same for you; and some will make you laugh. But I can assure you that all of the suggestions come from myself and other moms who have tried them and found them worthwhile.

In addition to sharing ideas that will create special, memorable, fun and loving moments with your children, I will briefly explore the magic that exists through amazing sixth sense connections between a mother and child. Whether you call it mother's intuition, maternal telepathy, or an angel's whisper — it exists, it is very powerful and it is fascinating.

To understand the full love, power and responsibility behind motherhood is awe-inspiring, and I wish you the very best on your unique and miraculous journey.

Creating Memories

Thanks for the Memories...

I feel so blessed to have a place
Where I can take my mind
Whenever tears start flowing —
I go far back in time.

To when my mom was here with me
Always by my side
There was no one else who cared as much —
Her tears fell when I cried.

I'm thankful for the memories
That fill my mind with joy
The times she took me shopping —
And surprised me with a toy.

The way she never let me leave
Without a hug and kiss
Her constant show of joyful love
Is what I truly miss.

And now I must make certain
That I create a place —
Where my children can go and think of me
When they can no longer see my face.

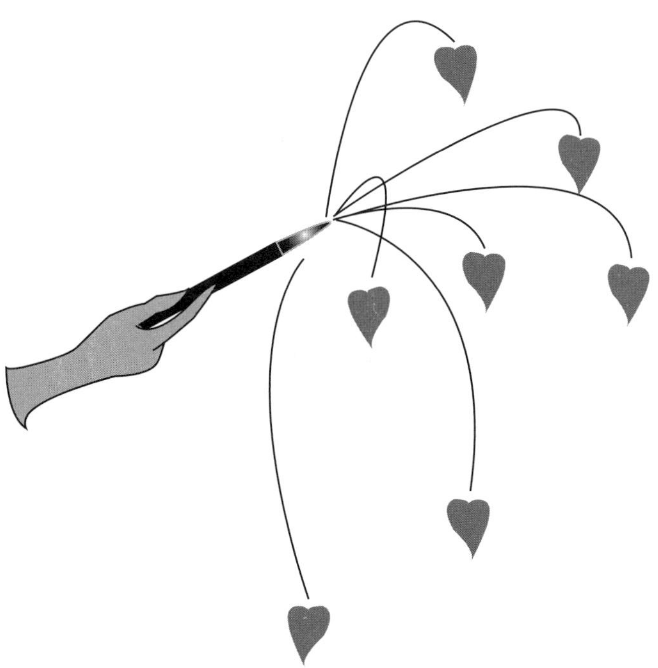

MEMORIES ARE MAGIC

You will find a lot of ideas in this book, but I decided to make this the first chapter because every idea you use will hopefully create good memories for your children. I also thought it would be fun for you to start by conjuring up your own precious memories.

Memories are, of course, created every day... without any conscious effort on our parts. Our experiences are stored away in our brain and when a smell, a song or a word reminds us of a certain one — memories of the entire instance flood our minds. I've often wondered why bad experiences are more readily remembered than good ones. Possibly because they make more of an impression. Imagine ways that you can make your child's good experiences more impressionable, and they'll have more of those to draw on when hurtful memories are unfortunately added in. Also, repetition is not only the mother of learning, but the mother of memory as well! The more you do something, the deeper ingrained it becomes. So why not put something that smells good on the stove every day, so the house always smells yummy when your children come in the door? Cinnamon toast is a good snack after school — so put cinnamon sticks on the stove one day (the smell lasts longer) — and put rolls in the oven (or bake bread if you're so inclined) the next day...and so on.

The following list is a collection of my own memories, as well of those of many others. My hope is that it will serve to tickle your own memory cells, remind you of things that have been tucked away for a long time and give you ideas about what memories that you want your own children to go through life with. And if you happen not to have been blessed with good memories of your own childhood — this is your chance to prove that history does NOT have to repeat itself. It is up to you to change your destiny, as well as the destiny of the precious beings that you have brought into this world.

The greatest gift that you can bestow upon your child is a happy and secure childhood — for that will be the foundation for how they view the world for the rest of their lives.

A Widow's Request

A very famous friend of mine did something that I shall never forget. After her husband lost the battle to cancer, she received dozens and dozens of beautiful floral arrangements and the charity of choice was blessed with generous donations. Fortunately for her and her young children, there was an enormous amount of support from family and friends, and her celebrity status provided for much public support. In her infinite wisdom however, she knew that soon people's lives would return to normal, and the support would naturally lessen. As much as she appreciated the outpouring of sympathy, she wanted something more for her precious children...something that would last. To accomplish this goal, she asked those close to her husband to write a story about him as they knew him. Stories from his childhood, college days, marriage, fatherhood, career adventures — anything they were moved to write. These requests were made privately, but also at the funeral in a touching and heartfelt request. She planned to put a book together for their daughters about daddy — full of the wonderful memories of those who also loved him. It would be a very special collection that they could look back on as they themselves went off to college, met the men of their dreams, started

cont.

families…all that their dad would love to have been a part of in this world, but now would be watching from above. They may not be able to feel his touch over the years, but they will certainly feel the magic of his existence through this ardent tribute to their loving father.

God gave us our memories so that we might have roses in December.

- James Barrie

Memories of Mom

Cinnamon toast and tea in bed whenever I was sick.

Popsicles in the bathtub.

The first day of school and we BOTH cried.

Saying a prayer together whenever we saw an ambulance or heard a siren.

Leaving a snack at night for the little people who I thought lived inside our television set.

The song you sang every morning to wake me up.

Laughing at ALL of my jokes, and no matter how many times I told you the one about the elephant on the fence, you still laughed each time!

The special notes that you used to put in my lunch box...and later in my care packages at college. I still look for them in my briefcase at times!

Playing for hours under the sprinkler in the front yard – until everyone in the neighborhood had joined in on the fun! You also provided the popsicles!

Being the hit of the neighborhood by dressing up on Halloween with us and going trick-or-treating.

Making us feel "rich" on occasion, even when you and dad were struggling.

The day we all went to that homeless shelter and dished out soup.

The Christmas morning when I heard my new puppy barking!

When I told you that the moon was always following me, and you said that God put it there to always light my path.

The time we sat on top of the van and watched the sunset over the ocean.

The morning that I dressed up in your high heels and glittery sweater, put on your make-up, perfume and hairspray and woke you with a surprise.

Family hugs.

Whenever I missed a line in a play or struck out in a baseball game, you always said that my performance had still been spectacular in some way. Like the time you told me that although I struck out, you noticed that my swing had become so much stronger that when I connected with the ball next time you were sure it would go over the fence!

Playing school and letting ME be the teacher.

Going to camp for the first time and being SO excited...until I got to the bus and realized that you weren't going with me!

Bedtime prayers.

Tea parties with stuffed animals.

When I asked you if I could live with you forever, and you explained how I would grow up and go to college and someday have a family of my own and a house of my own...but that those things would happen far in the future. Then when I told you that I would move in next door — you smiled that famous "I love you SO much" smile!

The time you got "woozy" blowing up my birthday balloons.

The time I overheard you saying a prayer asking that you would love my future husband and that he would love you just as much.

Watching you kiss daddy every day when he got home and the feeling of security that it gave me.

Feeding the ducks at grandma's.

The party you gave for the whole neighborhood when we first moved...just so I could meet the kids.

How excited you got when a whistle finally came out after you'd been teaching me how for weeks. Not to mention the first time I made a bubble with bubble gum!

The miraculous way that you made the worst night of my life into the most warm and memorable one with you.

The first time I flew on a plane and you asked the pilot if I could sit in the cockpit. I'll NEVER forget that moment.

I tried on your old costume from your first grade play...it fit and you cried.

Getting a gold coin from the leprechauns every St. Patrick's Day.

The way you always made me feel like a princess.

How I slept with you every night.

The sleigh bells that mysteriously rang outside on Christmas Eve.

The song that you made up for me using my name in every other sentence.

NEVER getting library books back on time.

The first time I beat you at Ping-Pong.

The first time I beat you at checkers.

The first time I beat you to the phone!

Our many, many shopping trips!

Pet store Saturdays...petting all of the puppies and kitties...and talking to the birds.

The time I took my shoes off after you told me not to and IMMEDIATELY stepped on a bee! Oh how I appreciated your not scolding me — not realizing that I'd already had a stinging lesson!

The time when we were all folding clothes in the living room and YOU put dad's underwear on your head! I'll never forget what you said..."If you can't beat 'em, join 'em!"

The famous bubble bath that I gave the dog.

When I got lost at the beach...and how long you held me when you finally found me.

Reaching for the sky on the swings when I was little — and your encouragement for me to do the same in college!

Your smiling face at school — many, many, many days.

Taking that art class together.

Taking dance together.

Mother-daughter (son) dinners.

Mysterious mail that always had my name on it.

The time you drove 200 miles to bring my favorite pillow to me when I went away to college...a great excuse to see how I was doing!

LENGTHY Monopoly games.

The game I loved when you would take an arm and dad would take a leg, and you both would say, "He's mine...NO...He's MINE. No, he's MY boy...No, he's MY BOY!!!"

The many Halloween outfits that you made for me....

The worst haircut of my entire life — when I refused to go to school for three days...and you let me stay home.

Picnics in the backyard.

Picnics on the living room floor.

Our airport trips to watch the planes take off.

Going to the art museum. (I was bored, but I loved being with you and lunch in the park afterwards!) It's funny though — I just love art museums now!

Planning family vacations.

The first time you painted my nails and I wouldn't let you take it off...which you never did...it just wore off and we did it again!

The time I got cut from the baseball team and YOU cried.

The vacation when we all went to __________. (This is a "fill it in yourself" memory for you!)

The way you would never answer the phone if we were having an important discussion or if I was upset over something.

The stories you would embellish as dad would tell them

by the fire on special occasions.

Roasting marshmallows and hot dogs on the fire.

The camping trip when we had to use the potato chip can as a toilet....

The infamous day when you "accidentally" bumped my former boyfriend into the community pool because he had made me cry too much.

The night of my first school play when you applauded the most — standing ovation included — even though I only had one word to say during the whole performance.

Surprise visits to grandmom's and granddad's.

Picking berries at Aunt ______'s. (Another fill-in!)

The time we caught about a thousand lightning bugs and kept them in a jar to light up the back porch for awhile. And then you told me we had to let them go because freedom was important to everyone — even animals.

Bike rides on the beach.

The night we all had to sleep in the car because there were no vacancies for hundreds of miles. It may have been uncomfortable for sleeping, but it was one of the most fun nights the family ever had together!

That time you made me turn my radio off and just listen to the waves when we were at the beach.

Helping me bake 50 mini-cookies in my Easy Bake Oven and taking them around the neighborhood with me.

The many compliments that you offered that started my days or evenings out right.

The time you let me eat my birthday cake RIGHT OUT OF THE PAN!

The time we switched places and I got to be mom for the day.

The look on your face the first weekend that I returned home from college freshman year.

The time you wouldn't stop applauding after the spelling bee.

I'll NEVER forget when we found that lost puppy, and how you were so diligent in finding its owner, reminding me how WE would feel if we lost our dog.

The way you always tried to include me in conversation, even with your adult friends.

The loan you gave me — and the gift you made of not making me pay it back after the first payment. I guess you just wanted to see if I would be responsible enough to start paying you back.

Reminding me of the miracles of God's creations on a weekly basis. Especially that butterfly that had the most spectacular wings I'd ever seen!

Not getting upset with me the day I came home muddy and sopping wet from playing in every puddle on the

way home from school on a warm spring day.
The way you STILL make me feel...still your pride and joy although I'm all grown up!

Always making my little crisis situations your high priority for problem solving.

The way you were always my best friend. I could ALWAYS count on you!

The way you let me keep my security blanket even after others said I should give it up. (Do you still have it?)

Tickling me to sleep almost every night.

Making my bedtime stories real with your animation.

Putting my name in the stories that were exciting...making ME the hero!

Taking us to fun places.

The time you took us to the Goofy lunch and arranged for him to single our table out.

Our first trip to "Tomorrowland" at Disneyland. It was so futuristic to think of the possibility of having picture phones, and now we can actually do it with computers! (You've got to get a computer, mom!)

The tea party with Mary Poppins.

Always setting the right example — even admitting when you were wrong.

Falling asleep in your lap as you stroked my hair.

Constantly reminding me, "I'd never know if I didn't give it a try."

Teaching me the joy of giving.

Always, ALWAYS hugging me before we parted. Even if you were just going to the store or I was going to play at a friend's.

Those constant reminders to think positive and FEEL positive.

The incredible love in your eyes when you held MY first child.

The first time I had Christmas dinner at MY house!

How you have always been there for me. In the middle of the night when I was scared as a kid, to the times when I just needed a decently home-cooked meal, to now — when I just want to feel like your little girl again!

All of those times when you gave up something that you wanted to do and opted for something that I wanted to do.

The thousands of times you said, "Shoulders back, chest out, stomach in...."

Every Christmas and Easter you stayed up most of the night before to make sure the day would be absolutely perfect for us, as tired as it made you.

The first time you told me that I had a guardian angel.

When my helium balloon flew out of my hands and I said it was okay because grandma would catch it in heaven...and you cried.

The fact that you have never broken a promise...except of course when you had to rush to the hospital to have my brother when you had *promised* to play cards with me!

Our many car trips and my famous lines that echo around the world..."Are we there yet? I have to go to the bathroom. Does the hotel have a pool?"

Always doing your very best to make my wishes come true...and still do if at all within your power!

The time you got a letter from the insurance company raising your insurance because of a speeding ticket that I got on the way back to college...the one I "forgot to tell you about...."

The many colds that you got because you came to EVERY ice hockey practice and game.

Family nights...bowling, Parcheesi, canasta, movies....

Meatloaf dinners on Thursdays.

The way you have always supported and loved dad.

Being the team mom every time you could be.

Driving my friends and me all over the place!

The many prayers that you have said silently on my behalf.

Letting me make my own mistakes.

The times you let me stay home from school even though I wasn't physically sick. I will always afford my children those "mental health" days as well.

The discipline you instilled in me.

The way you could always get me to laugh when I was angry...and still can!

The nights you stayed up with me until the wee hours listening to every word I said with compassion and empathy.

The fact that you have never lost the little girl inside you.

The first time all of the neighbors came over on Christmas Eve and you played Christmas carols on the piano and everyone sang. I never knew you could even play the piano until that night!

The way you never allowed me to say, "I can't."

Consider the past and you shall know the future.

- Chinese Proverb

The Whole World Is Magic... Through the Eyes of a Child

A Fresh Look

A child's heart overflows with joy
Their love is fresh and true —
Their eyes look clearly on the world,
Few tears have blurred their view.

Childhood is a special place
Where trust and love abound —
The smallest things bring happiness
Like puppies, hugs and clowns.

Remember how you saw the world
When you were only three.
Then close your eyes and fill your mind
With thoughts that set you free.

Clear away your worries
And rest in solitude —
Then look into your child's bright face
With refreshed gratitude.

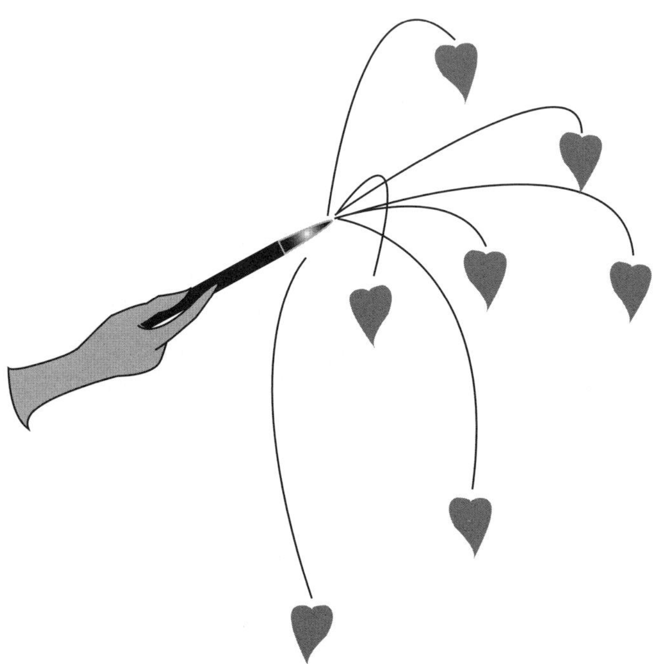

It's a Different World Through the Eyes of a Child

Take time at least once a day, to look at the world through the eyes of your child — rather than through your own. You'll be amazed at what you see. Often you will catch a glimpse of their childhood wonder, and sometimes you will see a particular situation differently — as viewed through their eyes. Part of the magic of being a mother is the bond that you have with your child that lets you know how he's feeling or what she's thinking. The key is to make sure that you act on what those feelings tell you. Your child will appreciate the occasions when you take the time to do so. Situations that seem unimportant to you may hold high importance to your child.

Kids DO say the darndest things, as Art Linkletter so beautifully pointed out to us on television and in his wonderfully humorous books — but sometimes what they say might be funny to you, yet serious to them. Mr. Linkletter tells of a six-year-old who, when told that he had no school because it was George Washington's birthday, asked if he could go to George's party. How priceless! However, our response to a comment like that should not be laughter alone. We would need to explain why he can't go, as well as why we were laughing. To them, they're missing a party if they're not told that there is no party — and they may even be hurt that we would laugh at them. Laughing WITH our children rather than AT our children is extremely important...and the difference between the two is very slight. I have been amazed at how many times my sensitive little children have asked why I'm laughing at them when that wasn't what I meant AT ALL!

When my oldest son was eight years old my husband and I were hosting a very big affair, in an elegant room of the Congress building in Washington, D.C. Since it was just a few weeks before Christmas, we asked that each attendee bring a toy for underprivileged children. We asked two charities to send a representative to collect the toys, and decided that it would be a golden opportunity for our son to experience the art and pleasure of giving. Therefore we asked him to give a short speech and present the toys to the charities. He wrote a wonderful little speech and sat patiently through the evening until his time came to speak and make the presentation.

One of the charities represented there was the Prison Fellowship Foundation. They were going to give the toys to the children of parents who sadly would be spending Christmas in jail. The other was an abused children's home. Of course I had read the speech that my son had written and was pleased and proud. The last sentence of the speech, as he wrote it, went like this: "I feel bad for those kids whose parents are in jail and hope that these toys will make them happy. I'm very happy that my mom and dad take such good care of me and that they also thought of taking care of so many other kids this Christmas too."

The problem was that he did not read it as he had written it...instead, his last sentence went like this: "And I'm so glad that I have parents who love me and I'm very happy that they're out of jail!" AAAHHHHHH!!!

You can imagine the looks on both my husband's and my face as 500 people looked at us and wondered when we WERE in jail...and why!!! I guess the shocked look on our faces cued the audience that we were innocent and they broke out in a roar of laughter that my son was embarrassed about for years. The first time I retold the story, he cried and left the room. I had no idea until that moment that he felt that way and it broke my heart. From then on I would tell it when he was not present. Not until recently, when we had a long talk about the difference between laughing AT and laughing WITH did he understand that the audience was TRULY laughing at his comment rather than at him personally. And now he tells the story himself and laughs.

Great movies have been made where the parent and child switch places and end up understanding each other MUCH better during the process. In the real world, however, all I can suggest is that you try to see things through the eyes of the child within you as much as possible. This chapter will give you ideas on how to see the world from one to four feet tall, and create an even closer bond between you and your munchkins!

In the interest of the theme of this chapter — two "special moment stories" will be shared instead of one. Because Ann Gallant did not want either of her sons to feel left out, and she has so many loving tales she could tell about them both, she wrote a story about each of them. As my mom used to say to my brother and me, "FAIR IS FAIR!"

Peirson's View

By Anne Rogers Gallant

I inherited many wonderful traits from my parents, but I never was quite thrilled about my head of tousled, curly hair. At its best it has always been out of control, and it is red. Throughout its existence, my long and unruly hair has been repeatedly wrangled in braids, arm-wrestled into ponytails, and generally confined to quarters by an array of barrettes, hairpins and other assorted devices. The goal was to keep it out of my face, and away from the population at large.

This truce served my childhood well as I danced, played, ran, swam, etc. I even took pride in the nicknames my mop generated — Cousin It, Veronica Lake, and even Medusa. I liked having a name for every hair personality, and I liked having a head with many personalities — depending on the humidity. Through my imagination, I could be a movie star, or dance the "Nutcracker." My hair became an integral prop for these make-believe fantasies.

As the years passed, I spent an ever-increasing portion of my life trying to straighten, fix, change and just plain deal with my rebellious red mane. The magical connection with my hair disappeared and eventually, my hair and I could not even keep our childhood truce.

One day however, my youngest son Peirson, who was four years old, came into my bathroom to

cont.

visit while I was dressing...as was his custom. (Mothers throughout the world know that the word "privacy" does not exist in our children's vocabularies!) I had just reached the "What shall I do with my hair today?" phase of the process.

As I furiously swept my hair down from its "circle" (what Peirson and his older brother Karl call my hair when it's wound up in a bun), I saw in the reflection of the mirror my precious little baby staring at me with a quizzical look in his eyes.

He suddenly exclaimed, "MOMMY! Are you a MERMAID?"

I turned around and looked into his tiny, angelic face. He was gazing at my red, unruly hair with a look of excitement and awe. "You are SO beautiful!" he continued.

As I scooped him into my arms to thank him for such a wonderful compliment, he said, "You must be Ariel, Mommy!"

I kissed him, and as I glanced into the mirror, the view was, just for a second, a cascading bouquet of fiery locks. And for a moment, I saw what he saw and it truly was magical.

My young son scampered away, but quickly returned clutching a fork in his little hand. He had remembered how mermaids comb their hair, and wanted to help.

Together, Peirson and I finished the job of "What shall I do with my hair today?" For the first time in years, it didn't seem like a struggle at all.

Mommy Is Always With Me

Also by Anne Rogers Gallant

In our family we always had something called a "there-there." Every family has one. It's that thing, a blanket, stuffed animal, bottle, whatever, that makes a baby (on up to an adult) feel better…just because.

Our oldest son, Karl, came home from the hospital wrapped in a sweet, soft, little white receiving blanket with satin borders…his future "there-there." As he grew it stayed with him always. He HAD to have it. As we waited for all of those incredible firsts, I was delighted one day when out came a word that to me sounded very much like "Mommy." Much to my chagrin it turned out to be "money." We weren't sure why or where it came from (although my late father had been a banker and we wondered if it was Daddy's heavenly joke to us). Whatever the origin, it soon became clear what a "money" was…it was Karl's blanket, his "there-there." From that moment on we never really used the word blanket again. I would even wake up cold in the middle of the night and say to my husband, "Honey, you've got all the money!" It is one of our special family words.

When Karl was very young I never left him. When I finally decided it was time to branch out, he would work himself up into such a state that

cont.

he would literally get sick at his stomach. It broke my heart, but I knew that I had to help us both get past this obstacle. The first time I left him with a babysitter was miserable. I can still see that tiny, perfect face peeking out of his "money" with tears streaming down it. Choking back my own tears, I told him that Mommy would be back soon. Then I wrapped his money all cozy around him and said, "Mommy is always with you."

Over the last few years I have watched with mixed, and often selfish emotions, as his young world has grown slowly, but surely, larger. At times, it seems as if he can't wait to get away from the nest. As any mommy knows, this is both traumatic, as well as the reason why we exist.

The very first time our increasingly sophisticated, then seven-year-old went for an overnight, I went to his room to help him pack. I wanted to make sure that something other than Legos, action figures and Pokemon cards went into his suitcase. When I walked into his room he was furiously stuffing his "money" into his bag.

He looked up at me as if he had been caught with his hand in the cookie jar. "I'm taking my money with me — do you think it's okay?" "Of course darlin'! You can take anything you want," I replied.

Then he said words I will treasure forever…"It will be good to have it 'cause it means Mommy is always with me." Once again, I choked back tears.

Well, he made it through the night, which is more than I can say for myself. I didn't sleep at all! But there have been many sleepovers since then. It gets easier every time — for him, not for me. It's all happening so quickly, but the one thing that never changes is that he always takes his money (now slightly frayed and worn from all the love) with him.

I am sure though, that if and when he ever stops taking it, somebody will find *me* looking like I've been caught with *my* hand in the cookie jar... stuffing his "money" into his suitcase because, "Mommy will ALWAYS be with him!"

The voyage of discovery lies not in finding new landscapes, but in having new eyes.

- Marcel Proust

When your child wants to talk to you, get down on their level. Kneel down so that you can look directly into their eyes, or have older ones sit on the couch with you.

When you say "wait a minute," it seems like an hour to them...especially if it DOES turn into an hour.

When you tell a lie, it teaches them to lie. Think about what is going through their little heads when you think you're telling an innocent lie to get out of doing something.

When they get an "A-"on their report card — don't ask why there's a minus — they're just proud of the "A"!

Don't just watch them play all the time — join in frequently. Reading a book as they play at your feet brings far less joy than joining in. The challenge is not just to baby-sit and make sure they're safe — but to interact and make sure they know you deem them a fun playmate.

Call a local pizza parlor and ask for a tour. It's best if you go in a group. The children will find it fascinating, and the pizza will taste even better as they talk about the pizza man who "created" it! You won't look at pizza the same way ever again!

Find ways to enjoy the things that your children find pleasure in — that you would otherwise avoid! I am amazed at how much my little girl loves roly-poly bugs. Her love of bugs in general and my intense dislike of them is the only difference that I have found between us thus far! However...I have learned to actually hold and examine many little creatures because I do not want to destroy her high value of them. And to tell you the truth...they are sort of cute!

A child's imagination is often the best place they can go to have fun. If your child has an imaginary friend, set a place for the friend at the table. If he is fighting an alien, hand him a cookie sheet as a shield. Find as many ways as you can to enhance their imagination by becoming a part of it on a daily basis.

A trip to the grocery store may be mundane to you, but to your child it can be an adventure. New people, so much to look at and GOODIES! If your child is old enough, let him find things on the list and bring them back to put in the cart. For younger ones, let them pick one item that you will buy for them while you're there. Have them look for the item as you venture down each aisle. In the meantime, let them help you with your list by asking who can see the next item first!

Remember — children learn the most through observation! If you want them to be kind, show kindness. If you want them to have good manners, be courteous. If you want them to appreciate learning, let them see you reading your own books.

What you DO...they will TOO...and their memories are phenomenal. The following is one of my favorite illustrations:

A three-year-old "big" sister constantly supervised her mother when she changed the newborn. After one rushed session, completed without the typical sprinkling of powder, the child corrected Mom: "Wait," she cried, "you forgot to salt him!"

Choose your battles wisely. Remember it's good for a child to feel that they can win once in awhile. As I watched my little boy writing in the steam on the mirror after a hot bath, I REALLY wanted to tell him to stop because it would mess up the mirror, it wouldn't dry clear...all of the things my mom used to tell me. But something in my mind stopped the words from coming out of my mouth, and I was never gladder. As he finished the heart and wrote, "I LOVE MOMMY," I decided I may never enforce that rule again!

Often we can learn from the eternal, innocent optimism of children, as the following story illustrates:

When a mother saw a thunderstorm forming in mid-afternoon, she worried about her seven-year-old daughter who would be walking the three blocks from school to home.

Deciding to meet her, the mother saw her walking nonchalantly along, stopping to smile whenever lightning flashed.

Seeing her mother, the little girl ran to her, explaining happily, "All the way home God has been taking my picture!"

Sit on the floor A LOT.

Teach your children not just to look...but to SEE.

Children see with their hearts, until they are taught to see only with their eyes.

- Anonymous

Enhancing the Magic of Childhood Fantasies

Childhood Magic

The enchanting world of childhood
Is in a mother's hands.
For there is a special magic,
That only she commands.

This magic is a special gift
That comes from God above...
Given when a child is born,
Then nurtured by her love.

Through wisdom and devotion
A mother guides her child.
Though laughter and enchantment
Are as important and worthwhile.

There are many happy moments
As our children go through life —
But when the disappointments come
This "magic" lessens strife.

Those warm and charming moments —
Ingrained in childhood years
Are a comfort when those troubled times
Bring sadness, grief and tears.

But most of all the magic
Soothes the heart and soul —
And cultivates the happiness
That is this life's true goal.

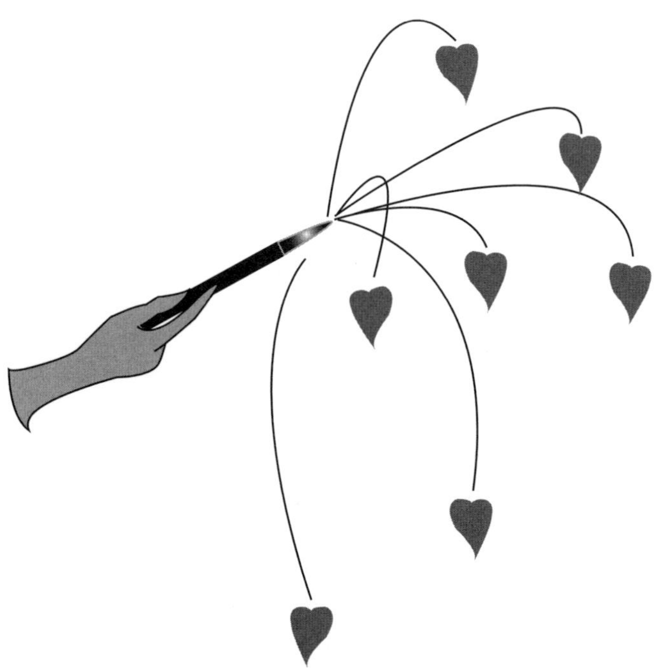

LIFE WITHOUT "MAGIC" IS LIKE A DAY WITHOUT SUNSHINE

Can you imagine growing up without having had a little magic to make the world a more enchanting place? Imagine the holidays that would never have been the same. Losing teeth would have just been painful...and the quarter that your grandfather pulled out of your ear would have lost its luster.

What about the happiest place on earth—Disneyland? How could it exist without "magic?" Belief in the magic of life is the key to enjoying it. However you define magic — have fun with it. From the magic of love to the magic of the hummingbird, the world is what you make it.

As suggested earlier, we are responsible for "creating" the world as our children see it. Our outlook on life will most likely become their outlook. So utilizing the magic that we possess to create magic in their lives is a gift that will last forever.

In this chapter we will explore magic that will let your child delight in the fantasies of childhood. Along with the traditional fantasies that come with the holidays, we will also offer ways to take advantage of the moment.

One such time occurred while our family was visiting Disney World, when my boys were ages three and five. After a long and very magical day, I was presented with a marvelous opportunity as we sat on the curb of Main Street and watched Tinkerbell fly down from the castle and then an amazing display of fireworks. When we got up to leave, Chase and Dane spied those eye-catching wands that look as if they are sprinkling color into the air. Unfortunately they had seen them in the hands of another child, and the vendor selling them had closed for the evening. They were very sad, but too tired to whine for long. I told them that oftentimes wishes came true at this magical place, and that maybe they should wish for the wands. They loved the idea and made the wish out loud to Mickey. The next day I awakened before they did and raced out to buy the two wands. I put them in a bag with a "note" from Mickey, and then placed them outside the door. The suite in which we were staying was two levels so when they awakened I had my husband keep them upstairs so that I could sneak downstairs to ring the doorbell and run quietly back to the couch. I yelled for them to answer the door, which they did with great enthusiasm. "We don't know anybody here!" yelled one. "Who could it be?!" cried the other.

When they opened the door and looked in the bag, their eyes got as big as saucers. "It's the wands we wished for! And there's a note!" Chase yelled as he ran over to me, "Read it, read it!" "WOW," I said. "It's from Mickey Mouse!" "What does it say, what does it say?" they screamed. "It says, *'Wishes really DO come true at Disney World...Love, Mickey.'*"

Fortunately I had remembered to supply the batteries so that the wands illuminated immediately before their eyes. "WOW," cried Chase," WOW," copied Dane. They were happily entertained the rest of the morning and repeated the story to everyone who would listen that day. It was a day that they, and I, will remember forever.

Brianna's Magical Land

By Lorena Serna

Throughout my life I have been afforded the opportunity to travel abroad extensively. During my travels I was able to meet interesting people and take part in the diverse cultures that these countries had to offer. However, these experiences pale in comparison to the majestic world my daughter, Brianna, has shown me. A world I once knew as a child, but had forgotten due to the inevitability of time. I consider myself blessed to be given the chance to visit this world once again with my daughter as my guide. Throughout our travels together we have seen fire-breathing dragons that are kind at heart, fairies with iridescent wings shimmering with all the colors of a rainbow and princesses who fall in love and live happily ever after.

Recently, I took my daughter on a picnic to a nearby wooded park. While lying on the blanket together we saw clouds transform themselves from the gases I have known them to be into ponies and puppies. We lowered our heads to where the grass around us became as tall as city skyscrapers and dragonflies soared above like helicopters. A bee buzzing around was no longer just pollinating the flowers, rather he was telling them stories of his adventures in valleys far away. We saw two squirrels playing a game of chase in the treetops overhead. Brianna informed me, with a seri-

cont.

ous look on her face, that they should be careful because the trees were so tall and they might fall and hurt themselves. Regarding this matter I sincerely expressed my agreement.

After we had eaten our lunch we went for a walk in the woods, with Brianna leading the way. I soon learned that Indians made the path we traveled on, a fact she pointed out after finding a feather that surely must have fallen from the headpiece of a great chief. Once we reached the lake we were greeted by jabbering geese who were arguing amongst themselves as to which one of them would be first to eat the bread crumbs from Brianna's hand. She made sure they all received equal portions, which included the smallest one who had missed out on a few because he did not move as fast as the others. On our way back through the woods heading towards the meadow, Brianna found a wizard's staff. She pointed out how this was a very rare find because it looked just like a stick and was often overlooked by those who could not tell the difference. She picked it up and proceeded to show me the proper way to hold it in order to get the most use out of its magic. While she held it in her right hand she pressed the end on the ground. She informed me that she had seen wizards do this to give themselves strength while on their long journeys.

A short time later a small butterfly fluttered up to my daughter, who by the way is fluent in the language of butterflies. It informed her that it was lost and afraid. As she held the butterfly on her index finger and brought it close to her face, she told it that she would help it find its way home. Amazingly, it sat quietly on her finger for the remainder of the trek. Brianna continued to reassure it that it was now safe and not to be afraid. When we reached the clearing at the edge of the woods, Brianna lifted her hand and the butterfly flew away. She then turned towards me and informed me that the butterfly had told her it recognized the meadow and knew its way home.

As I watched her waving goodbye to the butterfly, the child inside me understood – and the mother I had become rejoiced in the moment. These times are precious and I want to grasp onto all of them and hold them close. I know that she will have many more adventures throughout her life and all of her journeys will have a special magic. I am just grateful that, for the moment, she is sharing her magical world with me.

Magic is the study of intention. Teach your children to trust their inner guidance system — because they have the "magic" right inside of themselves!

- Stephanie Yeh

This chapter is for parents' eyes only...we wouldn't want to give away any secrets!

As long as children are continually reminded that the real magic lies within them because God lives in their hearts, having some fun with enchanting tales will make their childhoods that much more memorable....

Sprinkle green glitter around on St. Patrickís Day and leave a special gold coin for each child. Those leprechauns can be mischievous too!

Have a neighbor dress as Santa Claus and peek in the windows the week before Christmas. Have him ring sleigh bells outside to start the fun. I'll never forget my son yelling out of the sliding glass door as Santa slipped through our back gate, "Santa — I've been a REAL GOOD boy!"

Before your child sits on Santa's lap, slip him a note letting him know what items your child WILL be getting for Christmas. Then Santa can say a definite YES to those particular presents and your child will be thrilled and more convinced at Christmas.

Never forget the importance of the Tooth Fairy and the Easter Bunny!

When a member of the family or a friend gets sick, after saying a prayer for them, hold your child's hand, and tell them that they can send a magic thought to the person to make them feel better. Sending love CAN work miracles!

Learn a few simple magic tricks to amaze your children and their friends. You'll soon be the hit of the neighborhood!

Teach your children some magic so that THEY can amaze their friends.

My son went through a terrible period where he would have nightmares every night. After having tried everything, he spied a "dream catcher," in an Indian reservation store. He knew about them, because a friend of his had one. "Oh mommy," he said, "maybe it will catch my bad dreams!" I immediately agreed and prayed it would work (the REAL magic!) To my delight, he hung it on his top bunk, and informed me for the next week that the bad dreams had stopped!

ALWAYS throw a penny in a fountain and make a wish! With little ones, have them share their wish with you. Oftentimes you can make that wish come true — and what an impression THAT makes! I'll never forget a wish my daughter made. When I asked what she had wished for she simply said, "I wished that I'll be a good mommy when I grow up!"

Add a dash of love to every meal you make. Touch your fingers to your heart and then act like you're sprinkling the love from your heart onto the food. Be sure to tell your children what the special ingredient is!

When we traveled across country with three young children, a dog and a ferret — we were looking for every way possible to make the trip more magical, memorable and tolerable! Strictly by accident, I came up with the "magic window" — which kept my four-year-old entertained constantly throughout the trip. She asked if she could open the window one day, and I said "Sure!" But instead of using the button, she started pointing at the window with her index finger, and pulling her finger down. Almost by instinct, I moved my finger to the driver's controls and made the window come down with her finger as she directed it to open. She was so surprised and thrilled she squealed, "Did you SEE that?!" "Oh YES!" I answered. "You must be magic!"

Pick a star that's viewable most of the time and name it after your child. If you want it to be official, there is a company called Star Names (starnames@aol.com) that will officially register a star in your child's name (for a price). Every evening that you can see their star, make wishes on it — or talk about how incredibly special your child is — and how they always need to "reach for the stars!"

Have the Good Behavior Fairy visit your home on occasion. This fairy leaves treats for children who are especially well-behaved. It can be a balloon with a congratulatory note tied to the doorknob of their bedroom — so that when they wake up they have a fun surprise. Or it could be a small toy laid on their pillow so that when they pull down the covers to crawl into bed they spy it. Choose whatever your particular child would consider a reward!

Ask a friend to call or visit at an appointed (exact) time. Then when the telephone or doorbell rings, pause for a moment and say, "That's ________." Your children will definitely think you're amazing. Of course, you'll probably have to arrange it a few times to convince older children!

Tell them that YOUR wish came true when they were born!

Write a secret message that has to be read in a mirror to "decode." Guess-who-loves-you is a fun one!

When you have to be away from your child, give them a piece of jewelry, or other special item to "talk" to you through...and show them what you'll be using as well. A necklace works well. If your child can tell time, it's good to set a time when you both will send messages of love to each other — or "I can't wait until you come home" messages. Of course they can do it anytime they would like as well. My daughter was very upset one day as I was leaving (even though I was only going to be gone an hour!), so I looked down at her little heart necklace and I said, "Did you know that your heart is magic?" She stopped sniffling for a moment and said, "It is?" I had gotten her attention off the problem of my walking out the door! "The heart inside of you is magic, and so is the one on your necklace, because it is a symbol of the love that you have inside of you." "Really?!" "Yes," I repeated. "And if you want to talk to me, all you have to do is talk into that heart, and I will feel your love." "Okay," she said, smiling. "Are you going to talk to me?" "Of course," I said enthusiastically. "I will use my ring...alright?" "ALRIGHT," she said. Then I hugged her and kissed her and handed her to daddy. This time she waved and smiled.

Remember to teach your children the magic of thought! The age-old saying holds much truth...YOU ARE WHAT YOU THINK...and the earlier that your children learn this — the better they'll be at living it!

Dress up for Halloween, conjure up some surprises and make your house the talk of the neighborhood kids...and yours!

Have your children create "giving" lists as well as wish lists.

Remember to give the gift of time during the holidays. It is a wonderful lesson for your children that "things" are not as important as spending time together and performing kindnesses for one another.

The post office keeps letters to Santa for people who might want to answer the needier ones. Be the Claus family and buy some of the things on the lists and deliver them to the needy family. The smiles on their faces will be the best gift that you and your family receive all season.

Have the Tooth Fairy, Santa, the Easter Bunny, etc. leave little notes with the goodies. It makes them seem much more real!

As a birthday, Christmas, Chanukah or any other holiday present, give your child a year full of treats by making a coupon booklet listing one treat that they will receive each month. This way the gift will last all year (and the expense can be drawn out over twelve months!)

Don't forget to accentuate the magic of love as the greatest magic of all!

There are only two ways to live your life:
One is as though nothing is a miracle –
The other is as though everything is a miracle.
- Albert Einstein

Tender Moments

THE MOMMY MAGNET

I awakened this morning early
With a foot attached to my leg
As I tried to gently separate
Her little voice said, "Let's play!"

Then I sat up in the bed
As her hand slipped into mine
I smiled and squeezed her fingers
For we are always intertwined.

I stood up, stretched and felt her eyes
Looking into mine
Her arms outstretched — that "carry me" look
I lifted her and sighed.

We nestled in each other's arms
Enjoying a bottle and coffee
And then I felt my feet get warmed
By our adoring little puppy.

Suddenly I heard a cry
My six-year-old awakened
Down the stairs he ran to me
Still a little shaken.

He climbed across the dog
And up onto my lap
Blanketed with love
There was only one spot left.

I heard another door and spied
Another smiling face
My oldest walked in sleepily
And calmly took his place.

My husband came to say goodbye
And gave us each a kiss
He knew he left us happy
Together in our bliss.

The phone can ring, the chores can mount
My work can loudly beckon.
But nothing's more important
Than holding my precious children.

It's as if I am a magnet —
A power truly treasured.
For the closeness that I share with them —
One could never measure.

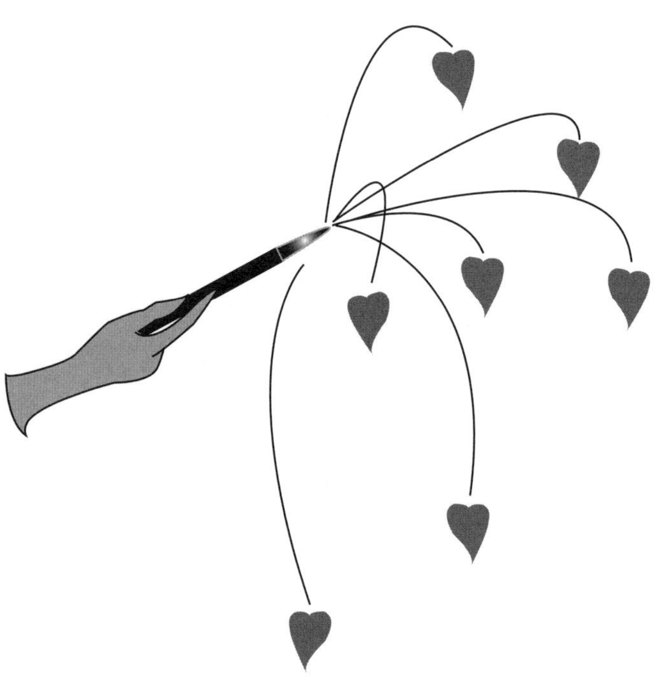

They're Never Too Old

I often tell my children that they'll *always* be my babies. Then, I proceed to tell them how their dad's mother still calls him her baby, so they will be my babies for a long, long time to come! However, it's hard to keep your little boy a baby once he starts playing ice hockey — and can run faster than you. Suddenly you feel like maybe you ought to honor his journey into manhood and stop some of those babying ways. It's tough to think about, but a mom's gotta do what a mom's gotta do, right? Well — almost. Take heart, moms. Here is a great story to renew your hope in keeping them your baby for a little while longer.

One night as I was tucking my ten-year-old into bed, he said, "Mom...will you sing me a song?" Taken aback that he would ask, since he had sort of ducked my kiss at school that day, I said, "Well...of course honey. What made you think of that?" I couldn't help but ask since it had been a few years since I had sung him to sleep. He said, "I was trying to get Astra [his little sister] to sleep last night and she asked me to sing a song to her. I asked her why, and she told me that that was how you helped her to go to sleep." "Do you remember me singing to you?" I asked. "Sort of...but I'd like to hear you do it again," he said softly. "I would love to sweetheart...," and so I began — to the tune of "Lullaby and Goodnight." "My little boy...is such a joy...and I l-o-v-e him dearly...." I continued to make up words as I went, and he seemed to put every word into his little heart. At the end he said, "That is so cool. Did you actually make that up as you went?" I said that that was how I always sang to them — telling them how I felt in my heart, and assuring them of mine and God's love. He was truly happy as he drifted off to dreamland.

A few weeks later, he came in while I was rocking my Astra to sleep...again singing to her. He stayed and listened for a few minutes and then disappeared. After I had laid her down he came into my room and asked me if I would rock him to sleep too. My heart filled with so much "mommy joy" that of course I leapt at the chance. I carried him into his room, where his little brother sat on the floor struggling to get his shoes off. I couldn't help but think that the moment would be lost, but I calmly turned off the light, and sat with him in a chair. Even with his brother as a potential teasing witness, he asked that I hold him like a baby. So I did...and once again, I made up a song just for him. I rocked back and forth — singing and looking into his face until his eyes started closing. As I struggled to get him into the top bunk, he again told me how cool it was. But this time, it wasn't only the song. He said, "Mom, you know how you were saying earlier how your love is like a blanket that covers us and makes us feel warm and safe?" "Yes," I answered, with my eyes filling up quickly. "Well, it was so weird because that's exactly how you made me feel as you were rocking me. It was like I was dreaming and I didn't want to move." He went on and on, and all I could think was that he was actually feeling the magic of the warmth and love that I felt for him. It was a mommy moment that I shall never forget. As I kissed him goodnight, I said, "Well, we'll just have to do that more often." He nodded happily and closed his eyes. And yes, I rocked his brother to sleep that night too. It was indeed a magical evening.

Tender moments are a natural part of mothering and most often come spontaneously. The suggestions in this chapter will offer ways to enhance the closeness that is cherished by every parent and child.

Forever, For Always, and No Matter What?

By Jeanette Lisefski

Our daughter Ariana moved from baby to toddler with her share of the usual bumps and scraped knees. On these occasions, I'd hold out my arms and say, "Come see me." She'd crawl into my lap, we'd cuddle, and I'd say, "Are you my girl?" Between tears she'd nod her head yes. Then I'd say, "My sweetie, beetie Ariana girl?" She'd nod her head, this time with a smile. And I'd end with, "And I love you forever, for always, and no matter what!" With a giggle and a hug, she was off and ready for her next challenge.

Ariana is now four and a half. We've continued "come see me" time for scraped knees and bruised feelings, for "good mornings" and "good nights."

A few weeks ago, I had "one of those days." I was tired, cranky and overextended taking care of a four-year-old, twin teenage boys and a home business. Each phone call or knock at the door brought another full day's worth of work that needed to be done immediately! I reached my breaking point in the afternoon and went into my room for a good cry.

Ariana soon came to my side and said, "Come see me." She curled up beside me, put her sweet little hands on my damp cheeks, and said, "Are you my mommy?" Between my tears I nodded my head yes. "My sweetie, beetie mommy?" I nodded my head and smiled. "And I love you forever, for always, and no matter what!" A giggle, a big hug, and I was off and ready for my next challenge.

The best and most beautiful things in the world cannot be seen or even touched. They must be felt with the heart.

- Helen Keller

When your child does something that reminds you of yourself when you were little, take time and share a story from your childhood with them.

Rock your older child to sleep.

Hold hands with your child out of love at times — not just when you're crossing the street.

Tell your children that your day just isn't right until they give you "morning hugs!"

Family hugs are also important. Get the whole family together and stand in a big circle and hug each other...often. (Remember the last Mary Tyler Moore show?)

Tickling your children to sleep or stroking their hair as they drift off to dreamland is just as important as reading to them before bed.

If your child still uses a bottle, enjoy a "ba-ba and coffee" as you snuggle together in the morning. The warmth will come from the heart as well as your coffee mug. For older children, pour them a hot cup of milk with sugar or hot chocolate.

Everybody gather under the covers with a flashlight, and read a story that touches the heart.

Sometimes the way we kiss our children when they're off to an activity or bed is like the famous Hollywood kiss on each cheek and "let's do lunch" attitude. Once in awhile when you hug your child, tell them that you can't let go...and make it a VERY long hug!

Use sign language for a secret "I Love You" sign, and use it often with each other. Put your thumb, index finger and pinky up, bend the other fingers down, and touch the same fingers on your child as you look deeply into their eyes.

Sing special songs to your children with their names and your feelings for them. I use the tunes to well-known songs and change the words. For example, I sing "Lullaby and Goodnight" with these words:

My precious girl
With little curls
She's so special to me...
I love her through and through
And she loves me too.
I'm proud of her
My sweet daughter
She is thoughtful and kind,
And I thank God every day
That He sent her to be mine!

When the moon is full, take a long evening walk with one of your children (take turns for one-on-one time). At whatever level that is age appropriate, talk about the meaning of the first walk on the moon, and what the astronaut meant when he said, "One small step for man — one giant leap for mankind."

Lay side-by-side on your big bed and hug each other close. Then roll with each other from one side of the bed to the other — sort of like a double cartwheel. You can hold your weight off of your little one with your elbows as you roll. My daughter and I did this once sort of by accident and now she asks me to do it every chance she gets! It creates lots of cuddly laughter!

Continue to brush your child's hair AFTER the tangles are out — run your fingers through their hair and massage their scalp gently.

You don't have to be close to your child to share a tender moment with them. If you have to be away, call them and tell them that you are hugging the phone and ask them if they feel it. One night my daughter was "talking" to her daddy on the phone. She hugged the phone to her heart rather than putting it to her ear. When she finally did put the phone to her ear I could tell that her dad had asked her why she had been so quiet. She said, "Daddy — didn't you feel it? I was hugging the phone since I know you're in there somewhere!" Then it was her father who was silent. "Daddy? Are you there?"

Lay with your child until he falls asleep. Bedtime does not have to be a battle if you take the time to soothe your child, making them feel secure and loved. Reading to them is wonderful, but being there as they drift off to dreamland is extra special. You are a much better security blanket than a piece of cloth!

Look deeply into your child's eyes…for at least ten seconds. Tell them that you can see right down into their heart, and that you like what you see!

Extend your "Mommy Magic" to families who might need a little extra love. There was a little girl in our old neighborhood whom I gave a hug to every day that I saw her…which was almost every day. As soon as she would see me, she would start running to me saying: "Mrs. Manary, you haven't had your hug from me today!" I don't really know who was helping who — but it was something that my own children came to understand the importance of.

I have heard, and believe, the old saying: "The best thing that a father can do for his children is to love their mother." Just remember, the reverse is true! Let your children know how much you love their dad!

Learn the art of giving your baby a massage.

Create a box full of hearts during February. Make 28 (or 29 during those special leap years!) red paper hearts, and help your children to think of ways that they can show their love to others. Then list one idea on each heart and put them in the box. The idea is to pull one out each day and perform the act of love.

Bathe WITH your baby sometimes. You can hold them easier, and it's much more fun…for both of you! Then use a great big towel that you can both fit in. The closeness is heavenly!

Instead of putting cold lotion on after a bath, put the bottle of lotion into the tub while your child is bathing. Then afterwards cover them with the nice warmth of the lotion and a big fluffy towel.

Put clothes right from the dryer onto your children when they come out of a bath or in from a snowy day of fun.

Take your child to the beach in the evening and sit quietly — listening only to the crashing surf.

Remember butterfly kisses and Eskimo kisses — and create your own special kinds of kisses! My daughter and I made up "cheek rubs" — and my sons have developed their own special handshakes.

Buy a comfy "snuggly" with wide straps…the kind that holds your baby in a little pouch. Some of my favorite memories are having had each of my children next to my heart even when I needed my hands to be free to do something else. In some cultures, a baby is never without body contact because touch is considered to be so important to an infant. When a mother has to put her child down, another woman puts the "pouch" on.

Tender moments…
One by one,
Will shine in the heart
As bright as the sun.

- Adria Manary

THE MAGIC OF HAVING FUN

Have Some Fun...Today

When we are blessed with a little one,
Life is filled with a new kind of fun.
The joy of childhood reappears,
As we remember our younger years.

And as we amuse our new generation,
We again feel that awesome sensation —
Of deep belly laughs and warm summer rains...
And realizing life, is simply a game.

A game to be played with the greatest of zest
And when it comes to playing
— our children know best!
So let down the barriers that life can create
And have fun with your kids, before it's too late!

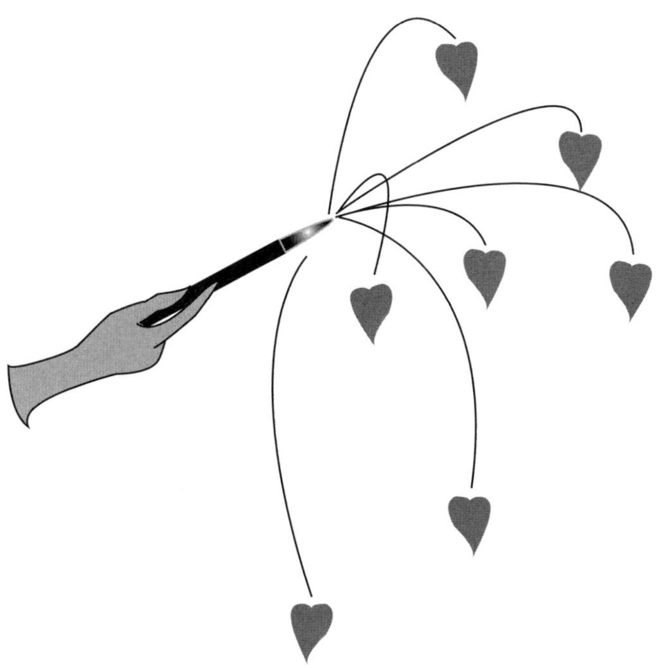

FUN: A POWERFUL FORM OF MAGIC!

It is a child's duty to have fun — and a parent's challenge to provide as much of it as possible! The fun that you afford your child is part of the magical world that you are continually creating for them. Of course they need to learn responsibility — but that too can be presented in a positive and fun manner. Life, in itself, is magical when you really think about it. And the more of it that you experience, the more magical it will seem!

Children are prone to laugh and have fun — it is their natural state of mind. I love it when my little girl starts laughing — just because her brothers start laughing — when she has no idea WHAT they're even laughing AT! Children do not have to plan fun like we do as adults...scheduling tee-off times, spending three weeks planning for a one-week vacation, buying the right clothes to play tennis in. Of course we need to provide fun activities for them at times, which is why I wrote this chapter. But if we follow their lead and try our best to make *everything* fun — then we're bound to have more of it than we could ever have planned!

In this chapter I will simply list lots and lots of ways to have more fun! Sometimes we do not provide as many fun options as we'd like to because it's too hard to prepare them or think of one at the moment. Therefore I hope that this list will make life a little easier for you in the planning department! Have fun!

I WILL NOW PULL A SMILE OUT OF MY HAT

By Linda Sharp

"It's time to wake up. You have to get ready and eat breakfast." Sleepy eyes slowly opened and I was greeted with the moans and groans of little people, still snuggled deep in their beds and full of that wonderful "sleepy warmth." Another school day had begun....or so they thought. As they trudged down the stairs for their morning bowl of cereal, they immediately noticed something very out of place. Or rather some*one* very out of place. There sat Daddy, who is usually long gone before they awaken.

A chorus of "What's up?" and "Why are you still home?" ensued. To his credit, he took no credit as he explained that Mommy had something special planned and had even made his boss give him the day off. As they gathered around my legs, I informed them that school would just have to get along without them for one day, and we were all going to a new amusement park! Oh joy! Oh rapture! Oh, hurry up and eat so we can go!!! What followed was a day that will stay in their memories and in my heart, long after they have forgotten fractions and spelling words.

I often joke that in addition to the illustrious title of Mommy, I am also a world class magician. I can produce giggles out of thin air and cre-

cont.

ate eyes that sparkle where seconds earlier there were tears. The sound of my children's laughter is truly the most magical music ever composed, and the smiles that I can create makes disappearing elephants pale in comparison. I take both of my roles seriously. These children regard me as a "force to be reckoned with" as their mother, but they also know I am a "force to be heckled with" and the biggest screwball around!

As with all great magicians, my children never know what is coming next. It may be as simple as being swooped upon from behind and finding themselves the victim of a "terrorist tickling" or being greeted with a made-up song about toilet paper when they come home after school. (You know you are a hit when you receive the child version of "Encore!" or "Again, Mommy, again!") I've been known to greet them at dinnertime with handwritten menus and a French accent, welcoming them to Cafe' du Momme', where the specialty is Ice Cream Sundaes. I've even been known to wear a disposable diaper on my head as a hat, just to make them smile while being tucked in. The point is that in a world they will soon know to be all too complicated, I take their fun seriously.

While today's magicians grew up studying the slight of hand and legerdemain of Houdini, I honed my "magic" at the foot of a master as well....my own mother. My earliest memories are of a woman who would get down on the floor and roll around with me till we were nothing but sweat and laughter. A woman who learned all the words to cartoon songs and would sing them with me in the grocery store. A woman who knew the truth behind the saying, "A child's job is to have fun." Even now, at my ripe old age of twenty-thirteen (you do the math), we still sing in the grocery store and do a mean version of the Weem-o-wack song.

Now I do not condone skipping school every week or singing about ...ahem...bodily functions in public, but creating joy and happiness is a trick that can be mastered by any mommy. All that is involved is being willing to drop a little dignity and let your kids see the child that can still play peek-a-boo from your soul. And while other so-called magicians may cut people in half and make the Statue of Liberty disappear, I prefer to use my magic to make my children double over and all their cares go POOF. Abracadabra!

It's kind of fun to do the impossible.

- Walt Disney

Serve breakfast in the bathtub when you're running late in the morning. A quick cinnamon toast waffle and a banana make a great finger breakfast! Your children will be clean, full and happy when they get out!

ALWAYS have a dress up box...for girls AND boys. And have plenty for visiting friends! I learned this a little late. My little boy went over to a friend's house when he was five and came home raving about the superhero outfits and animal masks that he had played with. As much fun as he had with the one that I then made up for him, I wish I'd thought of it when he was three. Oh well, his brother benefited earlier!

Make EVERYTHING talk. Of course the dolls and stuffed animals should have special voices, but other things can come to life as well. How about talking fingers or talking spoons — or better yet...talking food. When you're trying to get your child to eat some salad, you can have it say, "Oh please let me get into your tummy with the rest of my friends, Mr. Chicken Nugget and Mrs. French Fry. I know they miss me and I want to be with them! Don't you like being with YOUR friends?"

Special dates with mommy and daddy (separately) are important. One-on-one time is special, fun and often productive in finding out what's going on in their little minds.

Crazy rule-bending that doesn't hurt a thing is important in making your child understand that life is flexible. Eating the cake right out of the pan on their birthday (a family event...you can bake another for their birthday party) or starting a french fry fight (no mess, but all the fun of a real food fight) can surprise your child to no end and cause instant fun and laughter.

Teach your telephone number by singing it to the tune of "Twinkle Twinkle Little Star." Count the syllables — there are exactly seven...just like every phone number!

Hide their gifts on their birthday, and write poems and clues as to where the presents are.

Let one day a month be each child's special day — where they get to choose the family activities (within reason), as well as sit in the front seat (unless you have air bags), watch their favorite shows, eat their favorite dinner and dessert, etc.

Have a birthday party for your pet.

Host a tea party for your little girl's stuffed animals. Then host one for her friends — for no special occasion.

Create a family history scrapbook for the past year. Let your child draw pictures and add keepsakes such as ticket stubs. This can be an ongoing project that can fill in when boredom strikes!

Make up a special family holiday. Use your last name and add something fun like "SENSATIONAL SMITHS DAY." Use old white t-shirts and put the name on a shirt for each family member. Have a game where you commemorate the special aspects of your family. (For instance have each family member finish the following sentence: "The Smiths are sensational because...) Eat at the favorite family restaurant. Do whatever your family likes to do best!

When doing chores, make a game out of it by using a timer. They have to be done by the time the last grain of sand drops to the bottom of the hourglass!

Schedule family nights.

Have a different family member be responsible for the prayers each night, and tell what they are thankful for.

Have the children write an adventure story about the family (little ones can do the illustrations!). "The Mystery of the Lost Jones Diamond...."

Switch places for awhile — include the pets for real confusion! Your daughter can be the mom, her brother can be her, and you can be the parrot (after all you're *used* to repeating everything, right?!).

Encourage long-distance pen pals for them — by e-mail or snail mail. Write to the mothers of potential pals to get the ball rolling if they are too young or too embarrassed to do it themselves.

Choose a philanthropic endeavor that the family can do together. Sponsor a child through World Vision, Save the Children or another credible organization and have the child send pictures and letters each month with your sponsorship money. Or go to a homeless shelter for mothers and children and help serve meals. Or go to a nursing home and talk to the residents. They ADORE children.

Have a discussion about when THEY'LL be mommies and daddies. How many children are they going to have? Are they going to have boys or girls or both? What games are they going to play with them? How are they going to teach them right from wrong? Where are they going to live? You'd be surprised what comes out of this conversation. I know I was!

Children love to get wet — it's THAT simple! My daughter can play for an hour in the sink and not get bored. Water, plastic cups and spoons do the trick. Add a doll and you've added another half hour to that playtime. My older boys could play in the hot tub all afternoon. (I make the water warm rather than hot.)

Seek out the kind of bubble liquid that is edible. I've been a mom for over ten years, and I'd never seen it until my kids discovered this yummy and fun liquid at a Cracker Barrel restaurant. (You can find it everywhere now.) They just HAD to get some...and I obliged — thinking it was a pretty cool idea myself and couldn't wait to taste it! Needless to say — it was a big hit! (I think the grape flavor is the best.) One or two kids blew bubbles off of the deck while others tried to catch them in their mouths below. Deck or no deck, one child or ten — it is a great activity, and a perfect "video moment." A bonus is that there is no soap that sometimes gets in the eyes and puts a damper on normal bubble activity.

Pour regular bubble liquid into small containers, add

several drops of food coloring to each, stir and the "paint" is ready! Give each child several pieces of paper (for lots of wonderful creations) and a little bubble wand. Then the fun begins! Have them dip their wands into their favorite colors and blow the bubbles *directly* onto the paper. VOILA! Beautiful abstract prints and happy little artists! You might want to do this one outside, or cover an indoor area with an old sheet or drop cloth. (Remember the bubbles might get away!)

Put small tubs of water on a table or on the floor or ground. Put waterproof dolls or action figures in the water with other toys that the children can choose. This is a good time to explain what is waterproof and what can be damaged by water — and remember to cover what YOU don't want water on! After that, they'll be busy for a good while and water is easy to clean off of them and the area around them!

Arm everyone with squirt guns and join in on the fun as the moving target.

Give baths in the baby pool! Just fill it up with water as usual and squirt some Baby Bath solution into the water to make bubbles. Then let them play for as long as they want and when they get out, they're shiny clean! Fun for them, and less hassle for you to get them into the bathtub!

For some real water magic, put pepper in a glass of water and explain that each tiny piece represents a person swimming in the ocean. Then, tell them to watch what the people do when a shark's fin pops up in the middle. As you say this, put a drop of oil on top of the water and watch the "pepper people" scatter!

Okay—enough with water—I'm feeling waterlogged....

Put your favorite slow song on, pick your child up and slow dance with them.

Have fun with their food. Make shapes and characters out of sandwiches and pancakes as well as cookies. It makes lunchtime a lot more fun!

Teach your children to laugh at themselves. It is a very important quality that will give them peace and a better sense of humor as they grow up.

As we all know, spills and messes come with children. Instead of cleaning them up in disgust, try to lighten up once in awhile. It helps if you prepare for the likelihood of certain spills as well. For instance, let your child take their shirt off when eating chocolate ice cream...then when they spill it on their tummy say, "Mmmmm, chocolate tummy!" And "eat up" their tummy!

Go to the pet store and play with the puppies, talk to the parrots and wonder at the snakes.

Do something constructive as a family. It generates cooperation and teamwork, which are both essential elements of a happy home!

- Build a fort
- Create a videotape to send to relatives
- Paint a room that needs it
- Cook a special meal, with each person responsible for a certain part of it

- Make up a "continuing story" where the first person makes up a sentence, then each person that follows adds his own sentence to create the story. Make sure that someone acts as secretary to record it!

Go to the airport and watch the planes taking off. Have your child pretend that they're on one of them. Where are they going?

Build a fire and roast marshmallows.

Have a Christmas-in-July party.

JUST REMEMBER...BEING FLEXIBLE ALLOWS FOR MUCH MORE OPPORTUNITY TO HAVE FUN!

People are just about as happy as they make up their minds to be.

- Abraham Lincoln

Magical Wonders of Nature

Crayons Come from Rainbows

The wonder of nature
Is truly astounding
From the tiniest seed
To flowers abounding.

A child finds great pleasure
In God's mighty works
Wherever they turn
His magnificence lurks.

"Did God make my crayons?"
My little one asked
"No, crayons come from rainbows…"
In that thought he basked.

"I like the way He makes the clouds
And then puts pictures in them..."
I laughed inside and hugged him close —
His thoughts were oft such gems.

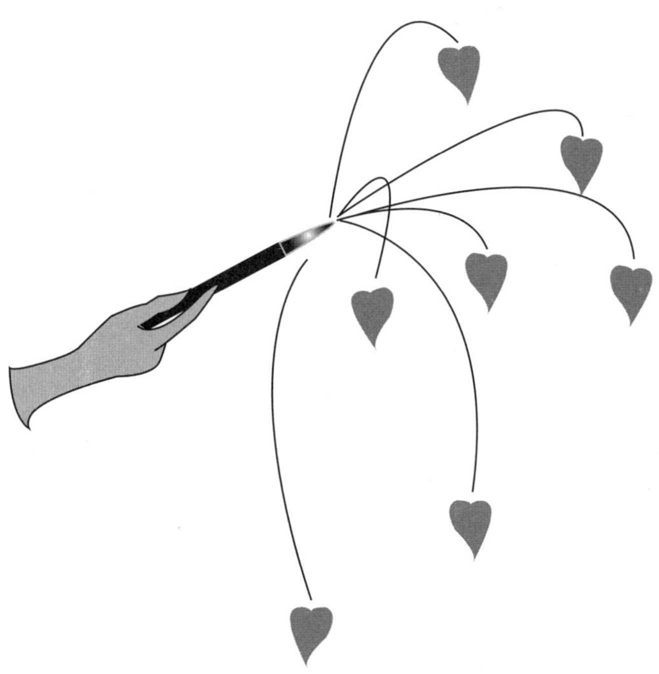

NATURAL WONDERS

A mother's magic comes with much responsibility, part of which is to ensure that her children are continually aware of the many *other* wonders of the world. A mere walk can turn into an enchanting adventure, if you simply take the time to point out the many tiny creations that God has placed here. Miracles happen every day — and children love to hear about them.

I once read a story written by a woman whose favorite memories of her mom were their daily trips to the mailbox. Why would such a routine chore become such a treasured memory? It was because her mother made those walks extraordinary with little stories about all of the little creatures on the way there and back. Think about it. The baby ant who became a hero. The caterpillar who turned into a butterfly. The fertile ground that they're walking on that will, or already has, produced pretty flowers or summer vegetables. And what if those stories included your child helping those little creatures? It's really easy if you let the child in yourself out for awhile and let her imagination flow free. After awhile, let your child make up stories too. Then, you can combine your stories by taking turns making up every other sentence of the story.

Let's take that idea a step further. What if there was often something IN that mailbox for them to look forward to? Arrange for mail to come to your child at least once a week. There are many "freebies" for kids. Or maybe a relative could send things...or mom could make up imaginary pen pals and tickle the computer herself if others can't! Then the trips would be filled with anticipation as well.

If it's a long walk in the country, great! If the mail comes to your door, make up another reason for a daily walk. Regardless of your own particular situation, you can always make your daily routine more fun by expressing interest in the nature around you. Walking the dog is another great reason to explore. Imagine how many friends he must make each day!

This chapter is full of ideas that will help you and your adored ones see the world as the truly magical place that it is. Just like when your children made Santa come alive again, you will be delighted at how they will breathe life into the world around you.

"MOTHER NATURE"

By Terry Lieberstein

I'm not a mom yet, but kids call me "Mother Nature." I've worked with children all over the country, introducing them to the wonders and joys of bugs, trees, animals, clouds and many other amazing things found in the natural world.

I guess you could say that I'm certainly a "mom in training," working with so many wonderful children. Two of my favorites are my nephews, Jake and Sam. We've spent a lot of time exploring together. Our favorite activity is what we call nature road trips. Our road trips are sometimes short, sometimes long, and sometimes in-between. Whatever we happen to be curious about that day, we move out to explore…singing, telling stories and playing as we drive. We have visited the beach to look for starfish in tide pools; the mountains to find fossils from millions of years ago; and even a quarry to examine rocks that were used by the local Native Americans to make paint.

The road trip that stands out in my mind was the visit to our local state park. Jake was eight and Sammy was five. We were walking down the path playing a hiking ABC game (where you search for things that start with each letter of the alphabet), when we turned the corner and there before us was a river. It was actually more of a

cont.

creek, but to Jake and Sammy — it was a RIVER. I've never seen two little boys get more excited! What could be more fun than a river with rocks of all different shapes and sizes on the banks?!

Sammy yelled, "Aunt Ter, can we throw some rocks into the river?" "Well, sure you can. That's where they came from, and that's where they'll be washed back to," I replied with a smile. I couldn't help but think how nice it was to be outside where you can say "YES" a lot more often! "Where will they end up?" asked Jake. "In the ocean?" "That's right!" I said enthusiastically. Then he said, "I guess everything ends up right where it belongs, doesn't it, Aunt Ter?"

Stunned into silence, I contemplated these wise words from my little nephew. I thought about how often I get too wrapped up in worrying about the future or the past…planning or regretting. And here the wisdom of the world spoke to me in the words of this wondrous child.

"Come on Aunt Ter, throw some rocks with us!" Sammy's little voice brought me back into the moment. "Okay, boys…here we go!" I threw the first and largest rock into the water…and the water fight that ensued was one to go down in the history book of precious moments!

If a child is to keep alive his inborn sense of wonder, he needs the companionship of at least one adult who can share it...rediscovering with him the joy, excitement and mystery of the world we live in.

- Rachel Carson

Help your child find a special nature spot for them to think, write in their journal, read, draw or just make pictures in the dirt. Make it special by marking it somehow. If your child is small, pick a spot near theirs for yourself, so that they do not feel more secluded than they want to be. During the winter, choose a spot by a window where they can look out upon nature if it's too cold. Point out how different the sky looks each day. How the trees change. How each snowflake is different.

Look at the leaves of a tree and find one that has a bite out of it. Who ate it? Explain how that leaf is like a french fry to a beetle!

Go strawberry picking and let your children eat as many as they can without getting a tummy ache.

Add an orange grove to your list of places to go on vacation (right below Disneyland or Disney World), when visiting California or Florida.

Swim with the dolphins! Sea World has a dolphin interaction program for children six years old and up as well as adults. It is an amazing experience and something they (and YOU) will never forget!

Catch lightning bugs and fill up a jar to make a lantern for awhile.

Check out a book at the library that identifies bugs, trees etc., and see how many your children can identify in your yard.

Spray paint on the snow! "Cool idea," don't you think?! (Pun intended). Just fill some spray bottles up with water and add a few drops of food coloring and VOILA — snow paint! The kids can write their names, decorate the front yard, and "dress" their snow people…whatever they want!

A treasure hunt is always fun. Remember "X" marks the spot! Draw a map for them to follow in the yard or in the neighborhood with hints along the way and a "treasure" at the end. A twist on this idea is to let older kids make the map for the younger ones. It's just as much fun for them to use their imaginations creating it as it is following it!

Make sure that rainy days are as happy as sunny days. When it rains, start the day out by saying, "Yeah — it's raining! We get to stay cozy all day!" And then sing this variation of "Rain, rain — go away…."

> Rain, rain — stay here today.
> The plants and trees are yelling HOORAY!
> We can play inside for awhile
> So you can make nature wear a smile!

Parks are key! Utilize their programs and playgrounds regularly! In addition, have your children become aware of keeping them pretty.

Sit quietly in the backyard and listen to nature sing to you and your children. Anyone who talks cannot stay for the concert.

Take advantage of your surroundings. If you live on the coast — go whale watching in the ocean and go to the beach for sunsets (or sunrises, depending on which coast you live on!). If you live by a lake — draw attention to the sparkles that dance on it at certain times of the day. If you live by a river — go fishing often! If you live in the mountains — go hiking! This idea may sound like common sense, but I lived in Washington, D.C. almost all of my life and never visited the White House!

Help the birds and entertain your children by putting out any kind of bird feeder. An easy one to make is to spread peanut butter on a pine cone and roll it in bird seed. Attach a string to it, hang it outside your window and VOILA — instant entertainment. If you live in an area where hummingbirds are, plant flowers that attract them. They ARE amazing creatures to watch. Be sure to explain to your children that it is "scientifically impossible" that a hummingbird can fly!

Plant some grass seed in a cup and watch it grow. It's easy, yet fascinating to a child, and it grows so fast, it seems magical! To make it more fun, draw faces on the cups that you plant in so that the grass looks like hair when it grows!

If you don't hate the computer, look up the natural wonders of the world and discuss the amazing aspects of each with your children. Of course books work just as well!

Help insects and birds find a new home by planting a tree...and explain that it will also provide more oxygen for the neighborhood!

If there is no lightning and thunder, let your child stand out in a warm summer rain and actually catch raindrops in their mouth. Join them if you can be that adventurous. They'll love the experience even more!

Take bread to a pond and feed the ducks.

Plant a "butterfly bush." It will attract butterflies like crazy and provide entertainment for all of the children in your neighborhood!

Draw your child's attention to the buds of flowers BEFORE they bloom, so that they can experience the birth of the flowers as the days go by. It makes flowers much more interesting.

Teach your children to appreciate the true beauty around them. The beauty of nature speaks to the soul, and to continue to call a child's attention to it is a precious gift to both of you!

Turn the radio, television and any other noise off when driving in your vehicle and encourage your children to enjoy the beauty around them in silence — for three minutes.

Go on an "ABC Hike." Find a path in a local park or natural area and see how many different things your children can find that start with each letter of the alphabet.

Have a "Mini-Safari" scavenger hunt to look for some of the smaller details that are not always noticed in the natural world. Items that can be included on the hunt list include: a spider's web, a caterpillar's cocoon, a leaf that has been nibbled by bugs, a drop of dew on a plant, a leaf with a fuzzy texture, etc. Add more items to the list that are appropriate for your environment.

Make a "nature bracelet." Affix a tape "bracelet" to your child's arm by wrapping a piece of two inch wide masking tape loosely around their wrist with the sticky side out. As they see things that interest them such as leaves, sticks, dirt and feathers, have them pick the items up and stick them onto the "bracelet." Remind them not to pick any live plants (or animals) for their decorations!

Take a "Micro-Hike." Have the kids "shrink down" to the size of an ant and crawl on their bellies along a micro-trail. Have them notice the micro differences between blades of grass, small rocks, etc. A magnifier or bug box can assist in their search.

Spray the hose so that the water falls into an arc shape to the ground on a hot summer day. You should be able to create a rainbow, which will REALLY make your children think you're magic!

Host a neighborhood "Nature Day." Ask everyone on your block to plant something that day. It can be a simple flower or a tree in honor of nature's role in making your street a pleasant place to live.

A person who cares about the earth will resonate with its purity.

- Sally Fox

The Magic of the Mind

The Power of the Mind

Teach a child when they are young
The power of the mind,
And you will see the benefits
As they begin to find…

That if they will "THINK POSITIVE"
And if they will BELIEVE —
Then there truly is no limit
To what they can achieve!

Fill their minds with happy thoughts —
Be there to hold their hand.
Then with God's help they'll reach their goals
As they shout inside, "I CAN!"

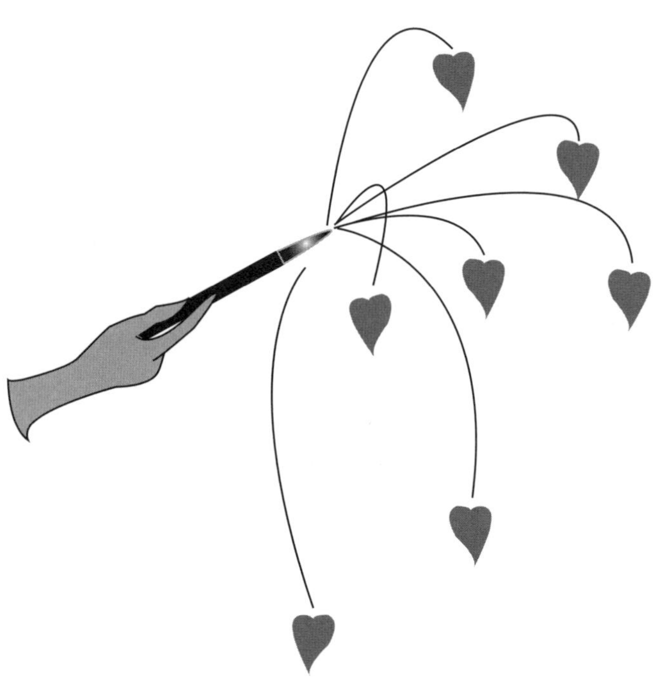

THE MIND... A TRULY MAGICAL PLACE

The mind truly is a magical place — a place where dreams are born, and plans are conceived to make those dreams come true. If we take the time to fill our children's minds with positive thoughts — they will benefit from the seeds that we sow for a lifetime. And if we teach them to visualize their goals at an early age — like professional athletes do...well, let's just say we might all be amazed!

One night my son Chase surprised me by telling me how he looked at his trophy shelf every night, and imagined a hockey trophy right in the middle! Hockey is his favorite sport — but there was every sport represented on his shelf EXCEPT hockey. It was also the only sport that he had played where the league only gave trophies to the top two teams...unlike the other sports, which gave participation trophies.

He visualized every night and played hockey every weekend. Finally, he had to go off to camp, and unfortunately had to miss the final two games. The team ended up receiving trophies, which were presented while he was gone. I picked his up — so that it would indeed be sitting on his trophy shelf when he returned home. It's hard to describe the look on his face that night when there was actually a trophy sitting right where he had imagined one!

One of my favorite stories is the one about the little girl whose mother took her little face into her hands every day, looked deep into her eyes and said, "You have greatness within you." Of course the mother wondered if what she was trying to impart was actually understood by her young daughter. That is until one day when she couldn't find her daughter. She looked and looked until she spied the closet door slightly ajar. Hearing her little girl's voice, she wondered whom she was talking to. As she moved toward the door, she noticed that their dog was in the closet too. As she peeked in very quietly, she saw her precious little girl face-to-face with her German shepherd. Her daughter was holding the dog's huge face in her little hands and repeating the words that she had heard so often... "Clyde," she said very seriously. "You have GREATNESS within you."

This chapter will offer a list of quotes to stimulate the mind of your child, either by quoting them directly or by paraphrasing them to impart important lessons. It will also offer a list of ways you can help your child to develop their mind.

ENCOURAGING THE CREATIVE MIND

By Linda O'Leary Sheetz

My daughter's first day of kindergarten was actually conducted as an "Open House Day" where both parents and children attended a "Teddy Bear Party." The children were to bring their favorite stuffed bears and introduce them to the teacher. When all of the precious bears were properly introduced, the teacher handed out copies of a cute little bear for each of the children to color — however they wanted.

As each child began to create their own little masterpieces, the mothers began chatting amongst themselves. Although deep in conversation, I was keeping an eye on my precocious daughter. I didn't think anything of the fact that she was holding her copied teddy bear picture up to the light and tracing her own version of the bear onto the reverse side of the paper. I knew she'd color it after she'd copied HER rendition of the picture onto the back.

However — the teacher was not in the mood to appreciate another way of approaching the assignment. I turned just in time to see her approaching my daughter with an angry and disapproving look on her face. I quickly stepped in, looked her straight in the eyes and said, "Isn't it incredible how *creative* Brianne is to have thought to hold the paper up to the light to trace a second

cont.

bear onto the other side? Now she'll have two bears to color!" The teacher's face quickly softened as she said, "Oh my gosh, I never thought of it that way. I was just about to yell at her for not following my instructions."

Brianne proceeded to produce one of the most uniquely colored bears in the class. It was the perfect color scheme for what she felt represented her favorite bear.

I couldn't help but hope that the teacher would be the one to learn the greatest lesson that day!

Whether you think that you can, or that you can't — you are usually right.

- Henry Ford

We can all remember the famous sayings repeated over and over by our dear mothers…

> "Eat all of your dinner, children
> are starving all over the world."
>
> "Your mother knows best."
>
> "Money doesn't grow on trees."
>
> "Cleanliness is next to Godliness."
>
> "Chew with your mouth closed."

The list goes on and on — but most all of them had value and are pearls of wisdom from our pasts…even though we got tired of hearing them. As corny as it may seem, however, repetition IS the mother of learning, so making sure that we bestow powerful thoughts upon our children — even in the form of silly sayings or insightful quotes — is extremely valuable in their learning processes. Here is a list to choose from when you need a little inspiration!

The first one is for you, Mom…

Cleaning your house while your kids are still growing is like shoveling your walk before it stops snowing!

- Phyllis Diller

If you can't say something nice about someone, don't say anything at all.

- Anonymous

The important thing is to NOT stop questioning.

- Albert Einstein

Hitch your wagon to a star.

- Ralph Waldo Emerson

Only those who will risk going too far can possibly find out how far one can go.

- T.S. Eliot

You can do it!

- The cheer of every mother

You must do the thing that you think you cannot do.

- Eleanor Roosevelt

It is far better to be alone, than to be in bad company.

- George Washington

You must first be a friend to have a friend.

- Anonymous

It's better to have tried and failed, than never to have tried at all.

- Anonymous

Look for the good in everything and you will find it.
- Anonymous

The universe is full of magical things, patiently waiting for our wits to grow sharper.
- Eden Phillpotts

Goals that are not written down are just wishes.
- Anonymous

We are what we repeatedly do. Excellence, therefore, is not an act but a habit.
- Aristotle

Wisdom begins in wonder.
- Socrates

It's not only what you say, but how you say it.
- Anonymous

Am I not destroying my enemies when I make friends with them?
- Abraham Lincoln

Obstacles are those frightful things you see when you take your eyes off your goal.
- Henry Ford

Well-timed silence hath more eloquence than speech.
- Martin Fraquhar Tupper

Opportunities multiply as they are seized.
- Sun Tzu

A pessimist sees the difficulty in every opportunity; an optimist sees the opportunity in every difficulty.

- Sir Winston Churchill

The only thing necessary for the triumph of evil, is for good men to do nothing.

- Edmund Burke

It's not the size of the dog in the fight; it's the size of the fight in the dog!

- Mark Twain

A child prodigy is one with highly imaginative parents.

- Will Rogers

Children are likely to live up to what you believe of them.

- Lady Bird Johnson

Proverbs:

He who lies down with dogs, gets up with fleas.

One falsehood spoils a thousand truths.

Each person is his own judge.

He who learns, teaches.

Starting is the hardest part.

Exuberance is beauty.

Wheresoever you go, go with all your heart.

When you throw dirt, *you* lose ground.

If you are looking for a friend who has no faults, you will have no friends.

He whose face gives no light, shall never become a star.

Better to light a candle, than to curse the darkness.

The more you appreciate it, the better it gets.

We will be known forever by the tracks we leave.

He who likes cherries, soon learns to climb.

He is a good storyteller who can turn a man's ears into eyes.

A teacher will appear when the student is ready.

He whose hand gives, receives.

He who aims at nothing is sure to hit it.

He who helps someone up the hill gets closer to the top himself.

He who persists in knocking will succeed in entering.

Encourage a child's perpetual sense of wonder. Buy a book like *101 Questions That Children Ask* and be prepared to intelligently answer questions like, "Why does a mosquito make you itch?"

A joyful and secure atmosphere in the home provides the roots for self-esteem. In addition, although we must protect our children, it is not necessary to scare them. It is our duty as parents to keep the terrors of the world away from their minds until they are prepared to deal with the thoughts maturely. Be careful what is on the news, for example. You might not allow inappropriate shows because of their rating...yet often what appears in the news is worse!

Have your children keep a dream journal. Whenever they have a desire to do something, have them write it down.

Children LOVE poetry. Recite it to them from an early age and they will be more likely to enjoy the art of writing it as they grow older. You can also use it to instill rules, phone numbers and various ideals that you would like to ingrain in their minds. Songs are also a good way of doing this. I taught my daughter our phone number by singing the numbers to "Twinkle Twinkle Little Star" (it works perfectly — seven notes = seven numbers). "London Bridges Falling Down" could go something like: How can I be kind today, kind today, kind today? How can I be kind today — I will find a way.

Discuss events in the news that your child can understand — and explain how they affect your family.

Be sure to include your children in some adult conversations. Ask for their opinion and really listen to their response. You might be surprised at what you hear!

Have your child memorize a verse, poem or short story — depending on their age — once a week.

Delight in the uniqueness of each of your children. With your encouragement they will not be afraid to be everything that they want to be!

The important thing is not so much that every child should be taught, as that every child should be given the wish to learn.

- John Lubbock

There's Real Magic in Feeling Special

THERE'S ONLY ONE OF ME!

"There's only ONE of me!"
My child once squealed with glee,
As I told him how unique he was…
And what he meant to me.

"No one has my nose!
And no one has my toes?
And NO ONE has MY mommy…"
Then the tears began to flow.

"Why thank you," I said.
As I laid him in bed.
Then I said a silent prayer
And kissed his tiny forehead.

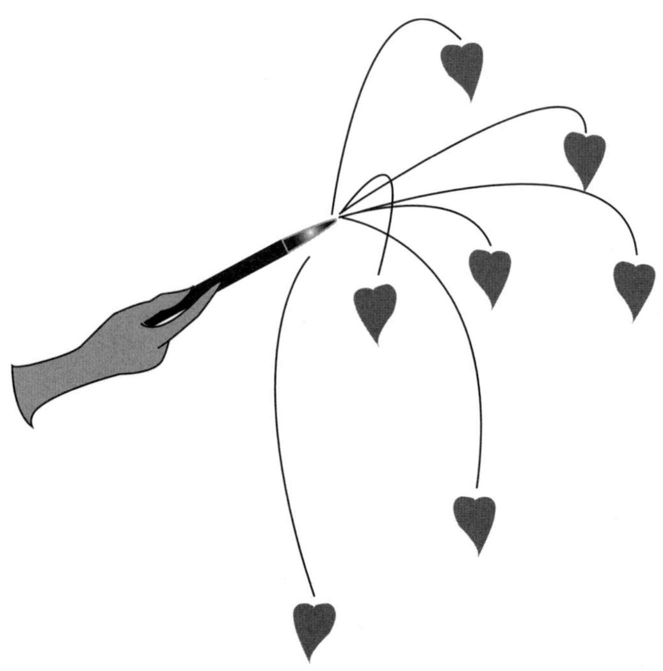

Feeling Like A Princess

If you tell your children that they are special — they will believe you. If you tell your children that they are not worthy, they will also believe you. If they are splendid in your eyes — it is likely that they will walk nobly out into the world.

When I was growing up, I was definitely the princess of the palace. My dad always called me his little princess — and one of my all-time favorite gifts from my parents was a pink "princess phone." Only later did I learn that the phone was actually put in my room for protection...in case of a fire, a burglar or some such other problem since I was a "latchkey kid."

My parents did everything in their power to make me feel special growing up. And when it was out of their realm of power — they fought hard to convince others of the importance of their goal. I can remember when my big brother made the Little League baseball team, and my mom made sure that I was the mascot — so that I could wear a uniform too. I also remember when she wouldn't take no for an answer when the Camp Fire Girls troop that I desperately wanted to be in said that they had enough girls for that particular group. How she got me in, I'll never know — she just said that they couldn't turn down a special girl like me! I can also remember when I was "picked" to be my former first grade teacher's aide — and was paid to help her after school. In actual fact, my mom had arranged this so that I would be supervised after school for the half-hour between school getting out and her arriving home from work.

They told me how I lit up a room when I entered it and how I had various special gifts. My mom told me that I had "peaches and cream" skin — even in the midst of those difficult teenage years when my skin was a real problem for me. I was applauded at recitals and given responsibility early because "I could handle it!"

My parents and brother were always the wind beneath my wings — and I feel that because of this I was thoroughly able to fly. What they said was sometimes true — and sometimes not so true. The point is that I BELIEVED what they said and lived up to their belief in me as best as I could.

We are all unique and have all been given special gifts. It is up to us as parents to help our children understand this — so that they will feel comfortable in traveling their own particular paths. We are all here for a reason — and as difficult as life can get at times — if we hold on to that belief from childhood through adulthood, our lives will be filled with the happiness that we were meant to enjoy.

Still Special... After All These Years

By Sandi Bruegger

My mom was a freshman in high school when she was thrown into the "real world" of marriage and motherhood. The marriage did not last and she soon moved to California in search of better things for herself and her new family. I chose to stay behind with my father, and have remained here for the last twenty years. Because of the thousands of miles between us, as well as the heartache, there was always a distance between us both physically and emotionally.

I met a wonderful man named John one fall, and by winter we were married. A few short weeks later, we learned of our pregnancy. There is always a part of you, no matter what age or situation, that feels the need to have the approval of your parents. This was a situation in which I knew I would never find that approval, however. My mom had always wanted my life to be better than hers. By that she meant I was to get a degree, be an independent career woman and maybe start a family in my thirties. She "could not" be a grandmother before age fifty! She was thirty-six when I became pregnant.

When I finally built up the courage to give her the news she reacted exactly as I had anticipated and feared...with utter disappointment. I

cont.

hung up the phone, angry and hurt, determined she would never be a part of our lives. After all, we had family close by that supported our baby and us. We'd be fine. We didn't need her. But a teary little girl's voice in my mind whispered, "Yes…we do."

We didn't speak often, but soon the packages began to arrive. First a few small things, and finally a crib and changing table set. I think it was the only way she knew how to say that she accepted her new role as Grandma, and that she had begun to respect my role as a mother.

When I went into premature labor at twenty-seven weeks, I attempted to reach her by phone to no avail. I finally was forced to leave a message on her machine, figuring that it would not be returned. The little girl inside of me was devastated. I lay in the hospital bed for hours, connected to countless IVs and monitors. I was trembling constantly from all of the drugs, combined with the terror of fearing my child's well-being was in danger. "I WANT MY MOMMY!" I screamed inside of my head. I fought the urge to dial her number again. John left to get a soda and I tried to concentrate on the steady blips that were my baby's heartbeat.

The sound of slow, reluctant feet entered my room. Sure that it was John taking his time getting back, I barked for him to hurry up. A hesitant hand reached up and slid the curtain aside. I had to blink the haze away several times, just to be sure I was seeing right. "IT'S MOMMY! MOMMY'S HERE — MOMMY'S HERE!" I cried inside of my heart. The little girl inside wanted to dance and sing. My mother stood there for a moment, tears in her eyes, unable to speak. And when she finally did manage the words — I learned a lesson in motherhood that I will carry with me for the rest of my life: "Remember, they just never stop being your baby…."

It is a fact that every child is special. Making them FEEL that way is one of the most important aspects of parenting.

- Adria Manary

Tell your child the story of the day they were born, and how there will never again be anyone born like them. If they are adopted, also tell them of the wonderful anticipation that you felt just before they arrived and how much love and effort you put into finding them…and how they were meant to be with you.

Special "dates" with mommy and daddy — separately. This is especially important if you have multiple children. This one-on-one time creates an environment where they feel comfortable in sharing feelings that might not otherwise come out in the normal, hectic pace of family schedules. It also creates distinct memories that they will put into the treasure trove of their minds!

Play Positive Roundtable. Sit around the kitchen table (or around the edges of the hot tub like we prefer!), and take turns offering one thing that each family member likes about the other members of the family. The first person says something that they like about every family member, and then the next person does the same, and so on. Sometimes it's hard to get started, but once it gets going, the results are positive and heartfelt feelings for the whole family. If someone is having a difficult time thinking of something for a particular person, be sure to help them quickly so that person does not begin to feel bad.

Do acrostic poems using your children's names. Make them meaningful and loving. For example, I wrote the following one for my little girl, Astra:

> **A** little girl that's such a pearl
> **S**o lovely in every way.
> **T**ries her best to please the world
> **R**eveling in every day.
> **A**n angel within her will always stay.

Make your child's birthday TRULY special...all day long. Start out by filling their room with balloons so that they wake up to a celebration. Put a candle in their pancake, toast or waffle — whatever their choice is. Then have the other children in the family do one deed each to make the birthday child feel happy or special. Let them decorate their own cake — maybe a separate one if there is a need for a "perfect" one for the party. Make sure to make the school celebration more than just cupcakes for the class if they're school age. A game about your child is often fun, with questions like, "What is Sally's favorite color?" Then the children who guess the correct answers can receive prizes, and the children get to know her better! Let the evening's festivities include a treasure hunt for the birthday presents — which provides for a longer time in opening them than simply ripping off the paper! Remember to fix their favorite dinner and serve it by candlelight!

Choose an area in which your child seems talented and make a point of telling them how gifted they are in that area. Use phrases like, "You certainly are a talented artist!" or "The kindness you showed in sharing with your friend was very special," or "I have never seen a more interesting rock collection. Maybe you'll be an archeologist!" (And then explain what an archeologist is!)

Make a family talent board, with pictures of each member doing what they do best — or maybe what they LIKE to do best!

Make sure that you let your children eavesdrop sometimes when you're "bragging" about their accomplishments.

Pick nicknames for each child that are special to daddy and different ones that are special to mommy.

Remember, compliments are important, and much more special if they are SPECIFIC.

Children hear "no" seven times more than they hear "yes." Explain that you must say "no" because you care about their safety and well-being — and that you wouldn't correct them if you didn't love them so much. In addition, however, find ways to say "yes" more often!

When they have achieved a particular accomplishment, hang a congratulatory sign up that they will see as they come in the door and have a special snack waiting for them.

Give flowers to your child. They're always picking dandelion bouquets for mom, so return the favor! I'll never forget the enthusiastic, wide-eyed response of my four-year-old when I brought her flowers after her first recital. "FOR ME?!" she squealed. "These are the FIRST flowers that I ever got!" Her joy penetrated my heart as she acted as though I had just given her a million dollars.

Teach your child the sign for "I Love You" in sign language. It can be your special secret code between each other.

Pull out old school work, pictures, cards and other memorabilia and make a scrapbook together, all about THEM. Discuss the value of each item as you place them into the book — describing how special the child is for having done such good work — and for having so many people who love them, etc.

Remember the dignity of your children. Never feel superior to them — because you are not.

Stop self put-downs immediately! Sometimes children get into a bad habit of calling themselves names or putting themselves down, saying things like, "I wish I was as pretty as Annie," or "Why am I always so clumsy?!" Bring up their good points and then ask them to tell you three things that they like about themselves. This should take the conversation in a more positive direction, and assure them that they are special.

Write letters to your child even if you're never apart. Writing your thoughts can be much different than speaking them as it offers time for reflection. Write about how you feel about them and how much you appreciate them, as well as complimenting them on things that they've done well. Leave the notes on their pillow, or somewhere they're sure to see them, or actually mail them. The words you write will be treasured by your children as they grow into their adult years.

When your child's feelings are deeply hurt, or when he is completely embarrassed about something, declare the rest of the day:

"Making [Child's Name] Feel Better Day!"

Have the whole family rally 'round! Buy them a special treat; have the other siblings write cards about what they like best about them; go out for ice cream; grant one simple wish that they have expressed in the past. Ease the pain of your child while it is still within your control! It will provide the understanding that they can ease their own pain as they grow older — and possibly the pain of others.

Give them periodic awards such as the one on the following page.

BEST CHILDREN IN THE WORLD AWARD FOR JUNE

TO

CHASE MANARY

FOR GOOD BEHAVIOR IN THE FOLLOWING AREAS:

1) For an EXCELLENT report card and making us VERY PROUD with his school awards.
2) Taking such good care of his sister at Universal and the Fair.
3) Making his bed every day.
4) Taking the trash out without having to be asked.
5) Doing chores when asked *without* exasperation!
6) For his sensitivity in showing his mother a great deal of compassion!

Make a recipe into "their" special dish. For example: Molly's Meatloaf, Sarah's Sugary Stars (star-shaped sugar cookies) or Sammy's Squiggly Sketi (spaghetti with curly noodles).

Always remember you are unique...just like everyone else.

- Anonymous

Cooking Up Some Magic

YUMMY SMELLS

Deep in my heart
Where my memories dwell,
Lives my mom in an apron
And yummy smells.

I'm thankful for cookies
And chocolate cake —
For when I smell these
Those images awake.

I am taken back in time
As I close my eyes —
And can almost taste the cookies
My mom baked with pride.

"Can I lick the bowl?"
My little one squeals
I'm jerked back to the present
By his wonderful zeal.

I look at his face —
All chocolate and smiles
And know that this moment
Will last him a good while.

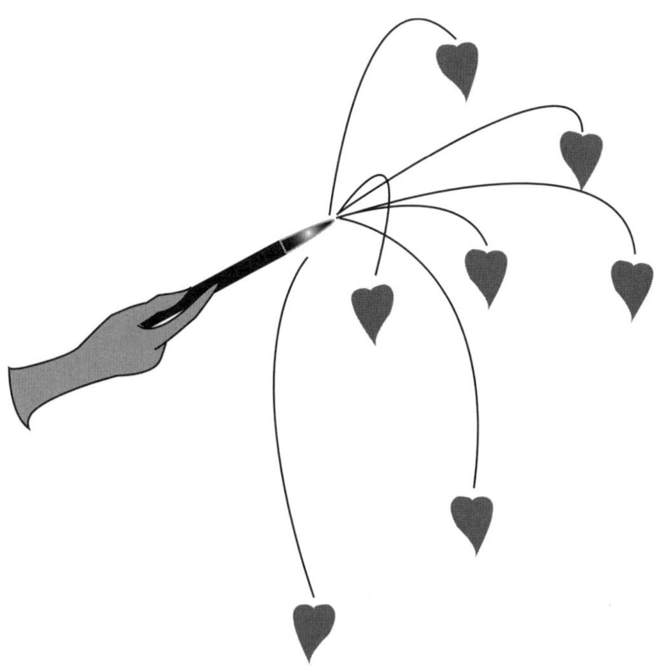

TASTES, SMELLS, MEMORIES

Our sense of smell has the power to evoke memories in an instant. Memories that were otherwise far from thought are conjured up so clearly that we are forced back to another time. The smell of oatmeal chocolate chip cookies in the oven takes me back to my mom's kitchen...watching her, helping her and waiting to eat the results. And when I eat pineapple upside down cake, although I've never tasted one as good as my mom made, I am still overwhelmed by a warm and cozy memory that I hope is never lost.

In writing this book, however, I had not included the importance of "kitchen magic" because — quite honestly — I am a terrible cook! Upon the suggestion of my dear friend Linda Sharp, and subsequent urgings from other mothers, I realized what an oversight that was, and thus included this chapter.

One fact that has remained true throughout the history of the home is that the kitchen has always been the center of activity. With the fast-paced society that we live in today, it is often at the kitchen table that we have our most insightful discussions and important family time. Even at parties, guests seem to gravitate toward the kitchen!

From holiday cooking, birthday cakes and fresh baked bread — to Jell-O jigglers and microwave cooking — making magic in the kitchen is a fun way to bond with your children as well as create memories that will last a lifetime.

In this chapter we will explore several fun recipes that are "children friendly" and mother approved! Of course, all recipes meet these requirements if you simply take the time to include your children in the fun. Often the simple act of letting your child crack the eggs can be the beginning of a plethora of enjoyable activities that will delight your children.

The Kitchen Magnet

By Val Acciani

We have kitchen magnets all over our refrigerator that hold priceless works of art, schedules, photos of happy times...doesn't every mother? However, the "kitchen magnet" that I am referring to here is the actual kitchen — AS the magnet.

My two vivacious little boys are always on the go...but when I go into the kitchen, my littlest one drops everything and is right on my heels. "Can I stir, mommy?" was, I believe, the first sentence that he ever put together. He had the motivation to use his words because he wanted to help mommy so badly. I will always call him "my little chef."

Having fond memories of special times in the kitchen with my own mom has been motivation for me to continue the same traditions with my children. When I was around ten years old I went through a difficult period of being the brunt of teasing at school. I would come home in tears almost every day, and there my mom would be — in the kitchen with ingredients for something yummy — ready for me to help create. The concoctions took my mind off my problems, and the time without radio or television gave my mom ample opportunity to hear what was wrong and share her wisdom with me. We shared many a

cont.

healing moment in that kitchen, and the bonding that took place over flour, eggs and sugar was a happy circumstance.

I now understand the many other reasons why these sessions were so important to my mom. Watching as my oldest counts out 80 marshmallows like a little miser — and then squash them all gleefully — turning back into the little boy I know! Letting my littlest crack the eggs (even though there may very well be a shell in the cake) and then watching as he walks like a monster to the sink — his hands covered in "GOO." And of course the many happy, chocolate-covered faces!

Of course the biggest reason I love our "kitchen time" is the special bonding that has occurred as a result of it. Holiday cooking is great, but when you make it an ongoing team effort, the fun is immeasurable!

The kitchen is always the happiest room in the house.

- Anonymous

FRIENDSHIP BREAD

The most important ingredient in this treat is *FRIENDS!* If you are starting this recipe without a bag of batter along with it, be sure to start at step six! Do NOT use a metal spoon or bowl for mixing and do NOT refrigerate. If air gets into the bag, let it out. A one-gallon Ziploc is best. It's normal for batter to thicken, bubble and ferment. Here are the day-by-day instructions:

Day 1 This is the day you receive the batter. Do nothing.

Day 2 Squeeze the bag.

Day 3 Squeeze the bag.

Day 4 Squeeze the bag.

Day 5 Squeeze the bag.

(Kids are great squeezers!)

Day 6 Add 1 cup all purpose flour, 1 cup sugar, and 1 cup milk.

Day 7 Squeeze the bag.

Day 8 Squeeze the bag.

Day 9 Squeeze the bag.

Day 10 Combine in a large bowl: batter, 1 cup flour, 1 cup sugar, 1 cup milk. Mix with a wooden spoon or spatula. Pour four 1 cup starters in Ziploc bags. Keep one starter for yourself, and give the other three to your friends along with a copy of these instructions.

Still on day 10…

cont.

Add the following to the batter remaining in the bowl: 1 cup oil, 1 cup sugar, 1 teaspoon vanilla, 3 large eggs, 1/2 teaspoon baking powder, 1/2 teaspoon salt, 2 cups all-purpose flour, 1/2 cup milk, 1/2 teaspoon baking soda, 1 large box instant vanilla pudding, 2 teaspoons cinnamon. Pour batter into 2 large well-greased and sugared loaf pans. You can sprinkle some extra cinnamon and sugar on top. Bake at 350 degrees for 60 minutes.

EASY FOREST TORTE CAKE

1 package Duncan Heinz Devils Food cake mix
1 package (3-oz) cherry Jell-O
3/4 cup boiling water
1/2 cup cold water
3 tablespoons cherry liqueur (optional)
1 package (4 1/2 or 4 3/4 oz) of instant pudding
2 envelopes Dream Whip topping mix
1 1/4 cups cold milk
1 can 21 oz. cherry pie filling

Prepare cake mix according to package directions, using two 9" round cake pans. A few minutes before the cake is done (follow the cooking time on the package), start boiling a 3/4 cup of water and mix with Jell-O until completely dissolved. Next add the 1/2 cup cold water and the cherry liqueur. (The liqueur is optional. You can just add an additional 3 tablespoons of water if you prefer.) Le Croix cherry brandy is a good choice. When cake has cooled about 5 minutes, remove layers to two separate dinner plates. Poke holes in both layers with tines of a fork. Next, slowly spoon the Jell-O mixture over both layers until all is absorbed. Cover layers with plastic wrap and refrigerate for two hours or overnight. When ready to frost, combine pudding mix, topping mix and milk in a small bowl. Beat at medium speed for 2 to 3 minutes. Using 1 cup pudding mixture, make a 1" high and wide ring around the outer edge of the top of one layer. Spoon the cherry pie filling into the center of this "corral," reserving about three cherries. Remove second layer from plate with a spatula and gently settle it on top of the bottom layer. Frost with pudding mixture, swirling it with your knife. Finally, put remaining three cherries on the top center. Refrigerate till ready to serve.

This is a fun and rewarding cake to make with your children. It is so delicious and you and your child will receive so many compliments that they will feel a real sense of accomplishment. Using a box mix makes this a user friendly recipe. Moms with little time and little cooking experience will find this is a no-fail recipe. The children love poking the holes in the cake and can do no harm ladling the Jell-O mixture any old way. Spooning the pretty cherries into the center of the cake is easy and fun, particularly when a few cherries miss the cake and meet a little mouth. Making swirls in this stiff frosting is easy and pretty. Finally, the chance for beater and spoon licking is a delight. You end up with chocolate noses and chins and big grins.

PUMPKIN PANCAKES

If your kids like pumpkin pie — they'll love these!

2 cups Bisquick
1 egg
1 1/2 cups milk
1/2 cup solid packed pumpkin
1 teaspoon cinnamon

1/2 teaspoon nutmeg
1 tablespoon sugar
1 spray can of whipping cream

Mix all together (more milk if necessary to make it the consistency of a regular pancake mixture). Pour onto griddle, desired size. (Remember silver dollar size is fun.) Serve with whipped cream. (And let the kids squirt the cream!)

HOMEMADE WONTONS

1 pound ground turkey
1 egg
1/2 cup green onion
1 1/2 tablespoons soy sauce
1 tablespoon corn starch
1/2 tablespoon sesame oil
3 shitake mushrooms, minced
A pinch of sugar
1 package wonton wrappers

Mix all together. Stir until blended. Lay wonton wrappers out and put 1/2 teaspoon of mixture into each one. From here follow directions on wonton package to fold. Boil a medium-sized pot of water. Cook the folded wontons 3-5 minutes. Drain and rinse. To serve, boil chicken broth and add desired amount of wontons — boil 2 minutes. Pour into bowls and sprinkle with more sliced onion if desired.

These are so fun to make, and kids love to eat them!

RICE KRISPY TREATS WITH A TWIST

(Double recipe)

1/2 cup butter or margarine plus an extra tablespoon
80 marshmallows
10 cups Rice Krispies cereal
1/2 cup peanut butter
1 cup chocolate chip morsels

Grease a 13″ x 9″ x 2″ pan. Add chocolate morsels with a tablespoon of butter. Heat (best in microwave) until morsels are slightly melted. Stir and smooth thin coat of chocolate across bottom of pan. Next, heat remaining butter in large saucepan over low heat. Add marshmallows, stirring until melted, then add peanut butter. Remove from heat, add cereal and stir until evenly coated. Press mixture into baking pan (use wax paper or spoon). Refrigerate until chocolate is hardened. Cut into 2″x2″ squares.

FORTUNE COOKIES

4 egg whites
1 cup sugar
1/2 cup plain flour
1/2 cup melted butter
1/4 teaspoon salt
1/2 teaspoon vanilla essence
2 tablespoons water
NON-TOXIC pen
Strips of plain white paper

Preheat oven to 350° F. Write down fortunes or messages on small strips of paper and fold them in half. (You can have a lot of fun with funny ones.) Mix the sugar and the egg whites and blend melted butter to the sugar mixture. Stir until the mixture is smooth. Grease a cookie sheet very well and pour the batter from a spoon to form circles around 2 inches in diameter.

NOTE: These cookies will spread so space them very well apart so that they do not join together. Cook for approximately 10-15 minutes and then remove from oven.

Place messages/fortunes on top of the warm cookie and fold the cookie over, and then over again, forming the fortune cookie shape. Cookies cool quickly and hold their shape.

EDIBLE FINGER PAINT

Light corn syrup
Food coloring (liquid works best)
Paper plates for mixing
Newsprint or other paper for painting

1. For each portion, pour 1 tablespoon (15 ml.) corn syrup onto paper plate.
2. Squirt food coloring into the puddle.
3. Mix and paint with fingers.

GRANDMA'S ORANGE COOKIES

1 cup shortening
2 cups sugar
2 eggs
1 orange (squeeze the juice, and grate the rind — reserve 2 tablespoons juice for the icing)
4 cups flour
1 teaspoon salt
1 teaspoon baking soda
2 teaspoons baking powder
1 cup buttermilk

Preheat oven to 400 degrees. Cream shortening and sugar thoroughly. Add eggs and beat well. Add orange juice and grated rind, mix well. In measuring cup, add soda to buttermilk. Combine flour, baking powder and salt. Alternate adding buttermilk and flour combinations, by thirds to creamed mixture. Mix well after each addition. Drop by tablespoons onto greased cookie sheet and bake for ten minutes, or until the edges are barely brown. Allow to cool completely before adding icing.

Icing

2 cups powdered sugar
2 tablespoons margarine
Dash of salt
2 tablespoons orange juice

Mix all together until smooth. Top each cookie. Icing will set up in a few minutes to allow you to stack the cookies in a container.

These are just a few to get you started on some kitchen fun!

Noncooks think it's silly to invest two hours' work into two minutes' enjoyment, but if cooking is evanescent, so is the ballet.

- Julia Child

MAGIC MANNERS

The Secret of Kindness

Kindness is the secret
To a person's peace of mind
Practice it on everyone
And you will always find —

Your own heart will be lightened
And your soul will be at peace
Even more than those you comfort
And those whose pain you cease.

So make a moment happier
For someone in your life
And make the world a better place
Where kindness conquers strife.

Sometimes the world seems scary…
Sometimes it seems so cruel.
But love can shine through darkness
If we mind the golden rule.

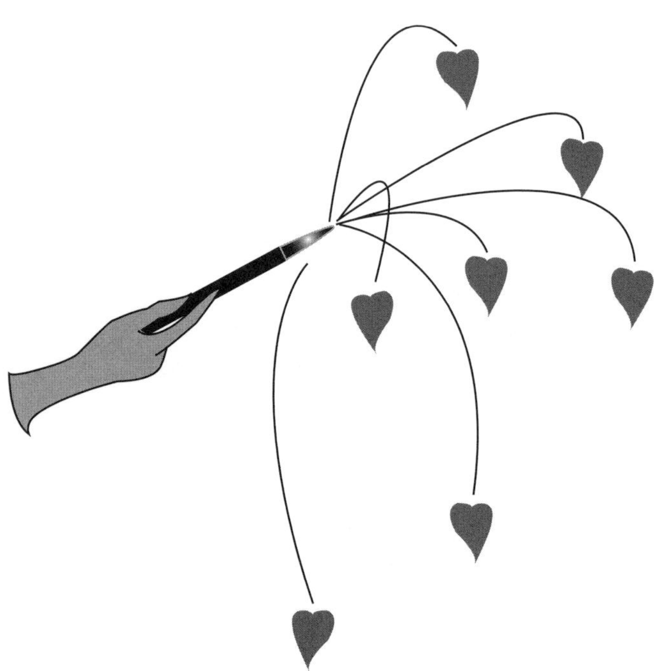

Beyond Please and Thank You

It is apparent these days that most parents and schools are doing a wonderful job teaching children to say please and thank you. After all, these are the "magic words." What is often missing, however, is an emphasis on the importance of courtesies and acts of kindness that go BEYOND these surface niceties. "Say the magic word," is heard over and over in kitchens and schoolrooms across America. What needs to be added is a reminder to perform the magic of kindness as well. In the "old days," having good manners meant more than just saying the right words. It meant not letting a door slam into the face of the person behind you, for example. Or making sure that someone was included in a conversation. Or watching children as they walked to school to see who might be left behind, and then encouraging the other children to walk with them the next day.

In a society that revolves around the great rat race, it was bound to happen. *We have finally given in to the rats!* I'm not referring to the problem of overpopulation. What I *am* referring to is the fact that the "rats" are taking over — in droves. They have been underground for a long time, eating away at our values and beliefs, but now they have gained enough momentum [and support...through apathy] so that they are rearing their ugly heads in public every day.

If you saw the movie "Ben," I'm sure you remember the last scene. I know *I'll* never forget it. It starts out with one innocent little rat...but by the end of the movie...well...let's just say it wasn't a pretty picture.

There is definite magic in being kind and having good manners. It can turn an otherwise gloomy day into one where the sunshine of your kindness has cast its rays into the life of someone less fortunate. It can simply make a person feel good. It can change a person's attitude toward you in a split second. It can open the door to opportunity. It will enhance your world and the world of those around you. The possibilities are endless.

In this chapter the suggestions and ideas will help you to show your children the importance of being kind, as well as the magic it can bring into everyone's lives.

Furby Has a Heart

By Letitia Baldrige

At the height of the "Furby" craze, during the holiday season, I happened to be standing in a toy store on New York's chic Upper East Side, awaiting my turn in line. Over in the corner, just watching, was a homeless mother, bare-legged, dirty and disheveled. I think she was in the store to keep warm, or maybe it was simply to allow her daughter to look at all of the toys. Her child watched the other children lined up with their caregivers, mothers and fathers, anxiously waiting to buy one of the coveted talking Furbies. Once or twice she said in a soft voice, "I'd really like one of those, too." Her mother quietly shushed her and told her not to be crazy, that, of course, she could not have one. The little girl's face grew sadder and sadder as she watched each furry character walk out of the store with someone else.

One of the private school girls, around ten years old, dressed in her pristine school uniform, saw and heard the little girl. When her mother finally received the treasured, wrapped Furby, she handed it to her daughter and paid the salesperson. As they walked out of the store, her daughter went over to the homeless mother's child, put the package in her hands and said, "This is for you." Then she hurried out of the store after her mother.

cont.

Tears came to my eyes. I had spent so much time writing about the need for children to develop a kind heart, about how we, as adults, should show them the way — and then I see a naturally and wonderfully kind child do an act right from her heart. There had been no suggestion from her mother that she give away her new Furby. There had been no conversation at all about it. She simply saw a peer with no chance whatsoever to own a Furby, it touched her and she reacted.

That child has what it takes to go a long way in this world. From what I witnessed, I feel confident she will achieve fame, fortune and success in every way...but most of all happiness. Kindness was in her heart, but surely her mother, father or someone at home helped put that kind of philosophy there. It just doesn't happen automatically, but how wonderful it would be if it were contagious.

Kindness in words creates confidence.
Kindness in thinking creates profoundness.
Kindness in giving creates love.

- Lao-Tzu

Whenever your child exhibits an act of kindness, not only acknowledge it — but also ask them how it made them feel. "Doesn't it feel good inside when you show kindness?" is a good phrase to use.

Pick a cause that appeals to the family, and do something to support it at least once a month. A few examples might be to take your pet to a nursing home; serve a meal at a homeless shelter; or sponsor a child through Save the Children or World Vision and not only send money, but also letters and pictures from the family.

Watch your children as they walk to school or to the bus. If a child in the neighborhood is always walking behind, encourage your child to think of something to talk to them about and walk with them sometimes.

Always say hello in an elevator.

Encourage your children to offer at least one sincere compliment a day.

Teach your children early that a promise IS a promise.

If you ever go to a poverty stricken area such as Tijuana,

Mexico, give your children bags of small apples that they can hand out to the needy children. My family did this and it was one of the best ways we've ever experienced in showing our children the value of small gifts to others. My heart swelled as I watched my little "pied pipers" handing out apples to these sad and needy urchins. As we walked through the downtown area, still being followed by expectant youngsters, my son said something that was far beyond his years. "You know what Mommy," he said, "some people want to be rich SO bad…and if they came down here, they'd realize that they are already rich!" He gave ME goosebumps — and HE learned a valuable lesson.

Teach your children good telephone manners. Think about what a welcome surprise it is when you call a friend and the child answers with good manners. Phrases like, "May I ask who's calling?" and, "Just one moment please" are simple — yet will set your children apart as children who have shown good manners.

Remember — a kindness a day keeps your own blues away.

Teach your children to encourage others rather than discourage them.

Have your children become "door monitors." Every time they go through a door, explain that a good door monitor looks behind to make sure that the door does not shut on someone coming up behind them.

Have your children write thank you notes for special acts of kindness that are shown to them as well as for presents.

If an elderly person lives in the neighborhood, suggest that your child help them once a week by taking out their trash, raking leaves, shoveling their driveway, etc.

Encourage kindness between siblings. Suggest that they each do something nice for each other at least once a week that is above and beyond their normal behavior. Perhaps doing their sister's chore because she has a project due at school the next day.

Have daddy help the children to understand ways that they can be kind to mommy. Perhaps playing quietly when she has a headache or offering to perform a chore without being asked. How about helping mom in with the groceries?

Put out a bird feeder to make the winter easier for our little feathered friends.

Teach your children to *look* for ways to show kindness. Things like helping a senior citizen into the car, offering to carry something for a person whose arms are full, offering their seat to an elderly person or a pregnant woman, or helping a mother with a stroller through a door.

Be a good example. If you are kind to others — so shall your children be.

Take flowers to a nursing home and have your child pick a resident to present them to.

Ask your child about the kids in their class. If there is someone who seems unpopular, encourage your child to be particularly nice to them — and protect them from the mean remarks of others.

Have your children pick out toys that they no longer use and instead of just taking them to a collection place — take them directly to an orphanage so that they can see the happy faces of the recipients.

Tell your children how much you love their smiles — and how important it is to smile at the people around them.

Pack some extra goodies in your child's lunch box to share with their friends.

If someone new moves into the neighborhood, have your child come with you to welcome them with a fruit basket or flowers from your garden. And if there are children — have your child show them where the park is, etc.

Remind your children to ALWAYS return a favor.

My son's fourth grade teacher had the whole class write down what they liked about each child in the class. Only good comments were allowed. On the last day of school, she presented each child's list of compliments to them. It was a very positive experience for the kids. Ask your child's teacher to try this.

Although it is important for children to understand that performing an act of kindness will be returned tenfold, it is also important that they understand that the act in itself is what brings joy to the heart.

Encourage your children to see through the eyes in their heart…rather than through the eyes in their head.

A loving heart is the truest wisdom.

- Charles Dickens

Magic Potions for Sick Children

Ice Cream Please...

It's awful being sick...
UNLESS you are a child!
For that is when your every wish
Is granted no matter how wild!

"Ice cream please — then Jell-O...
That is what I want...
For breakfast, lunch and dinner!"
To the store the mother jaunts.

"This is a magic potion!"
The mother says with hope,
That the little mouth will open
So the "meds" can help them cope.

Fluffy pillows, more TV,
Yummy treats and mom's caress.
Though the body may be aching —
The attention is the BEST!

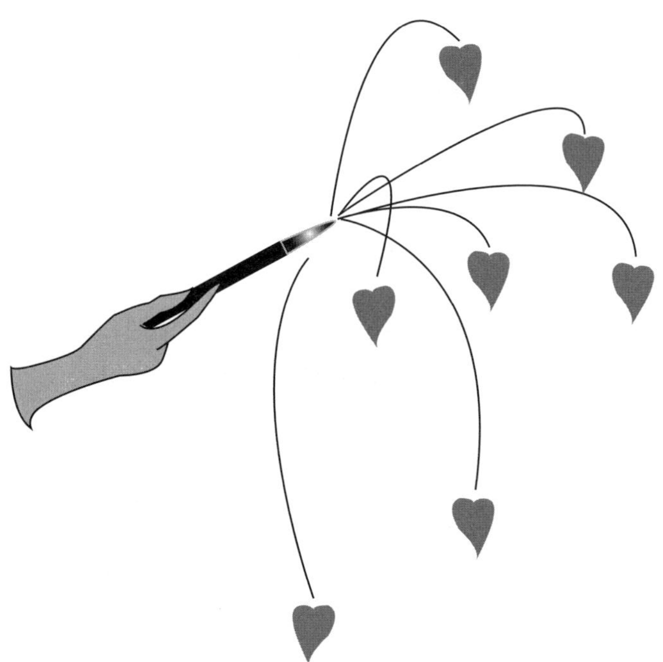

Cinnamon Toast and Tea

Powerful lessons in compassion are ingrained in children from an early age when they experience the tender devotion and caring of their mother when they are not feeling well. Cinnamon toast and tea come immediately to my mind when I think back on the days of my childhood when a sore throat, cough and stuffy nose would keep me home from school. Ah yes…those uncomfortable yet cozy days on the couch — propped up on fluffy pillows, a Kleenex box by my side and the television tuned in to "I Love Lucy" reruns. I even remember one time when my brother made my Barbie and Ken dance on the back of the couch to make me laugh…a rare and appreciated performance. Oh and the ICE CREAM….

Best of all, of course, was that my mom was by my side constantly. Of course when the illness is more serious, it's no fun for anybody. However even then, the show of love and concern can provide a sense of warmth and love that will last a lifetime. I can remember being extremely ill as a teenager and every time I opened my eyes, my mom was right there…sometimes sleeping…but always RIGHT THERE. Nobody likes being sick, but at least for a child, the experience can be one of reassurance that they are the most important person in the world and that making them feel better is the absolute top priority for their mom! The hectic pace of the world stops, and the child is shown in no uncertain terms that their well-being ranks above anything else.

I truly believe that the acts of compassion that we show our children when they are sick are valuable lessons of love. One time when a bird flew into the large glass window in the back of our house, my little boy wanted to bring it in, put it on a pillow and feed it Jell-O. Then he said, "Oh mommy, he's HURT. Let's make him comfy and rub his head."

Probably the best "potion" for a sick child is being curled up in mom's lap, nestled in her love — but I hope that the ideas in this chapter will help to comfort your children when you have to get up to make the Jell-O.

"I Couldn't Love You More If I Tried"

By Suzan Schweizer

All of my memories of Mom are enveloped by her constant, unconditional, never failing love. I actually had trouble adjusting to life as I entered school and found — to my confusion and hurt — that everyone didn't love me unconditionally.

Her love manifested itself in many ways, one of which was her warm and loving care when I was sick. In fact, being sick was a treat in our home. I actually felt guilty and questioned if I was really sick at times or just looking for the comfort and cocooning that my parents always gave. Mother would always make me a nice warm bath, and afterwards she would have fresh sheets right out of the warm dryer. I would crawl into bed and lay on the bottom sheet as she "made the bed" right on top of me, letting the top sheet gently float down in a comforting caress. Then came the cosseting of milk toast with sugar, Seven-Up, sherbet, custard, Jell-O…in other words — anything I wanted. I remember her saying, "I couldn't love you more if I tried." Her love was the best medicine of all!

Being sick isn't so bad when you have a mommy.

- Tommy
(four years old)

Have a special "feel better" snuggly (a pillow, stuffed animal or something soft) on hand when your child is sick or feeling blue. Keep it in a special place for whenever they need it. Tell them that it is a magic pillow that will make them feel better if they hug it.

Tell your child that whatever part of their body is hurting, you're feeling the same hurt in yours…because you truly "hurt" for them.

Hold your child's hand and tell them to squeeze it every time it hurts and you will send your special healing through the palm of your hand.

A child usually does not want to stay in bed (unless they are extremely ill) because they feel isolated in their room. Make an especially fluffy, comfy bed on the couch near you — or if they must stay in a bed a distance away, give them a special bell to ring for whenever they need you.

Have all of the family members make special cards for the sick child.

Always play their favorite quiet game with them.

A hot water bottle (not too hot!) is always comforting.

Help them make a list of fun things they are going to do when they get well — and write down your best guess for when they'll be able to start doing the things on the list.

Make them hot tea and cinnamon toast — or whatever makes them feel warm and yummy. Whatever you choose, serve it EVERY TIME that they are under the weather. It provides a wonderful warm and fuzzy memory of comfort.

If no one has called to see how they are, call a couple of relatives and friends without your child knowing, and ask them to call back to ask how your child is doing and let your child speak with them.

Remember — laughter is still the best medicine! Rent a funny movie, let the tickle monster attack, or put a diaper on your head. Do whatever it takes to get a smile out of your precious little patient.

Make stuffed animals talk, telling your child little stories about when "they" were sick.

A soothing song can brighten the day for a sick child. The following story was an extreme yet wonderful case in point....

Like any good mother, when Karen finds out that another baby is on the way, she does what she can to help her three-year-old son, Michael, prepare for a new sibling. They find out that the new baby is going to be a girl, and day after day, night after night, Michael sings to his sister in Mommy's tummy.

The pregnancy progresses normally for Karen, an active member of the Panther Creek United Methodist Church in Morristown, Tennessee. Then the labor pains come. Every five minutes...every minute. But complications arise during delivery. Hours of labor. Would a C-section be required? Finally, Michael's little sister is born. But she is in serious condition. With siren howling in the night, the ambulance rushes the infant to the neonatal intensive care unit at St. Mary's Hospital, Knoxville, Tennessee. The days inch by. The little girl gets worse. The pediatric specialist tells the parents, "There is very little hope. Be prepared for the worst." Karen and her husband contact a local cemetery about a burial plot. They have fixed up a special room in their home for the new baby, now they plan a funeral.

Michael keeps begging his parents to let him see his sister. "I want to sing to her," he says.

Week two in intensive care. It looks as if a funeral will come before the week is over. Michael keeps nagging about singing to his sister, but kids are never allowed in intensive care. But Karen makes up her mind. She will take Michael whether they like it or not. If he doesn't see his sister now, he may never see her alive.

She dresses him in an oversized scrub suit and marches him into ICU. He looks like a walking laundry basket, but the head nurse recognizes him as a child and bellows, "Get that kid out of here now! No children are allowed in ICU." The mother rises up strong in Karen, and the usually mild-mannered lady glares steel-eyed into the head nurse's face, her lips a firm line. "He is not leaving until he sings to his sister!"

Karen tows Michael to his sister's bedside. He gazes at the tiny infant losing the battle to live. And he begins to sing. In the pure-hearted voice of a three-year-old, Michael sings:

"You are my sunshine, my only sunshine, you make me happy when skies are gray...."

Instantly the baby girl responds. The pulse rate becomes calm and steady. Keep on singing, Michael.

"You never know, dear, how much I love you. Please don't take my sunshine away...."

The ragged, strained breathing becomes as smooth as a kitten's purr.

Keep on singing, Michael.

"The other night, dear, as I lay sleeping, I dreamed I held you in my arms...."

Michael's little sister relaxes as rest, healing rest, seems to sweep over her.

Tears conquer the face of the bossy head nurse. Karen glows.

"You are my sunshine, my only sunshine. Please don't take my sunshine away."

The girl is well enough to go home! Woman's Day magazine called it "The miracle of a brother's song." The medical staff just called it a miracle. Karen called it a miracle of God's love. A few weeks later, Michael's little sister was baptized at the Panther Creek Church.

One should not stand at the foot of a sick person's bed, because that place is reserved for the guardian angel.

- Jewish Folk Saying

Holding On to the Magic When Tragedy Strikes

Life Goes On

Life is full of tragedy
But hearts are made to heal.
The key to peace is coming back
From life's frequent ordeals.

A child's sweet soul is tender
To be treated gingerly.
Yet it is also given strength
In times of tragedy.

A mother's heart lends comfort —
Her hand security.
Her confidence in God's wise plan
Gives children certainty…

That life goes on regardless
Of whatever pain is felt —
And that it's up to them to thrive
No matter what they're dealt.

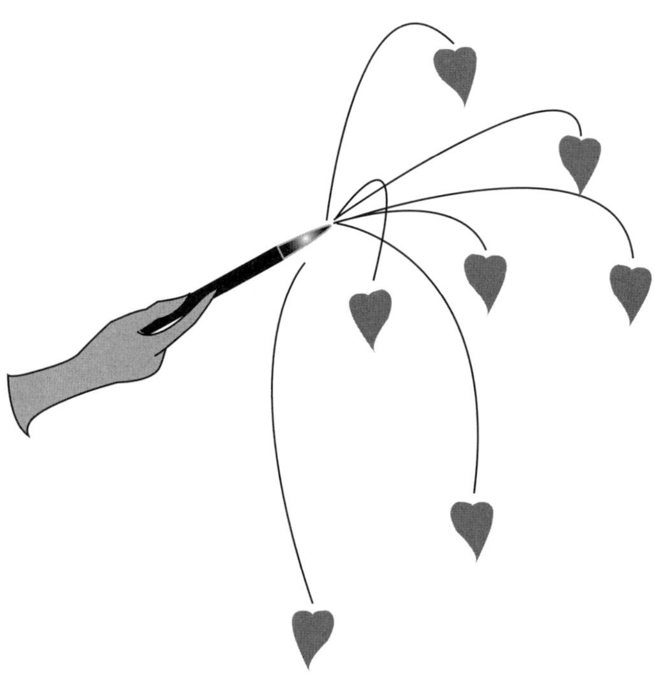

FINDING THE LIGHT IN TRAGEDY

When tragedy strikes at home, the family glue thickens. Suddenly it's the little things that matter. What DOESN'T matter is often what mattered MOST the day before! I believe that it is of the utmost importance to include our children in this transition — and help them to understand why things and feelings are changing so dramatically. Whether it be a physical or an emotional crisis, within our immediate family, or within our community of family and friends — our children are affected as much as we are, and oftentimes even more. Therefore, it is also important to let them see how we express our feelings and in turn let them express theirs.

On April 29, 1993, I lost my dear mother to cancer; ten months later my dad died of the same cruel and merciless disease; six months after that my first grandmother passed away; and shortly thereafter I had to break into my second grandmother's apartment when she would not answer the door...only to find that she too had joined the rest of my cherished family in heaven. It didn't end there, however. When we returned home from my second grandmother's funeral, we received another dreaded phone call. It was my husband's doctor. The test results were in. Our fears had materialized. He too, had cancer. The period of grief that I experienced during this period and beyond at times seemed insurmountable. The treatment and recovery period for my husband and family at times seemed never ending. But I was thankfully able to hold on to the magic of the lives that remained — and the life that we were fighting for.

At times I would hide to cry, because I felt that my children had experienced enough of the emotions of life. But I was often reminded that they wanted to be there for every tear. One day I was talking to a friend on the phone and began to cry. Not wanting my five-year-old to see yet another episode of sobbing, I took the phone into the hall and sat on the floor. As I explained to my friend how I longed to hold my mother's hand just one more time, my precious little son came around the corner and put my hand into his. With his other hand he stroked my hair — taking my headband off — I'm sure trying to relieve the headache that I had also complained of. He sat there on the floor with me until I got off the phone, and continued to sit there with me in silence until the tears stopped coming. It was the deepest display of compassion that I have ever experienced. At the tender age of five, he had soothed my sorrow in a way that many adults are not capable of.

The point is that it was good for him to have the opportunity to take care of mommy. At least he could be there and see that he could do something to help — rather than be at a friend's home trying to play, while in fact worrying about what was happening at home.

This chapter will gently offer ways to hold on to the magic of being a mother in the midst — and the aftermath — of grave adversity.

Holding Grandma's Hand

By Tamara Amey

When my beloved grandma died after a long and painful illness, it was very hard to say goodbye to her, yet we all agreed that it was a blessing to see her relieved of her pain. Grandma required round-the-clock care and we brought her home to live out her remaining days in familiar surroundings. At first, it was difficult deciding how much of this should be shared with our 12-year-old daughter. As it turned out, Kyla became one of Grandma's caretakers — helping turn her crippled body, rubbing lotion into her dry, fragile skin and even helping change her diapers.

As Grandma took her last breath, surrounded by her family, Kyla was by her side, holding her hand as she passed from this life. She became the parent as she hugged and comforted my father as tears fell from his face. While this was such a painful time for our family, I was very proud of my daughter's maturity and acceptance of this life event. Death is never easy to explain to our children, but letting them share in your grief is a healthy and important step in the healing process. We all miss Grandma very much — but have wonderful memories stored in our hearts by which to remember her. And Kyla will always feel a special part of the final memory that shall be felt in the hearts of the family forever.

When something bad happens, hearts open up from all around. The key is to keep your own heart open so that the love that comes can heal.

- Lea Hilburn

No one goes through life without the pain of losing someone close to them, dealing with sickness — or the many other hurts that life deals us. However, we must always strive to "make lemonade from lemons," and teach our children to do the same. It was important to me to include this chapter because no one knows when tragedy might strike, and one is never prepared at that moment. So although I pray for the well-being of every reader of this book, I want each of you to know that there is magic here — even in tragedy — when you need it most.

When a death occurs...

- Have the child involved write a letter to that person. It will help to let them communicate things that they may not have said, or may still not understand. Read the letter if appropriate, and help them to work through their concerns.
- Let them go to the funeral if they want to. The experience will provide them with some closure.
- Let them choose the flowers that they would like to put on the grave or send to the funeral home.
- Encourage them to put something in the casket that they've made or something that is special between themselves and the person who died.

- Have pictures at the funeral home that are of happy moments in the person's life.

When a pregnancy is lost and your child(ren) have been aware of the baby, it is important to think of what they have lost as well. Your loving reassurance that they are STILL a big brother or sister, even though their baby is in heaven, will help them cope with the loss and give them something much less scary than the baby just disappearing.

The following may not seem as severe as true tragedy, but in the hearts and minds of children — it is probably their first, and therefore gravest tragedy thus far:

- When a pet dies, even the smallest of them, have a proper funeral and burial. Let your child say a prayer and lay flowers on the grave. Please — don't flush their dear little goldfish down the toilet.
- When a friend's pet dies, encourage your child to show the proper compassion. Even if it was the neighborhood pet snake that you are glad to be rid of — think of the child who loved it.

Remember — your children can't wait. Of course you need time to yourself to grieve — or to heal. But your children need you continually. I can remember when my mom passed away, I realized a few months after her death that not only had I lost my mom…but to my dismay…my children were losing THEIR mom. It gave me great reason to find help and cope with my grief in a healthy way that would include my children rather than exclude them.

If someone close to your child has passed away, try reading the following "advice" from the Carmelite Monastery, in Waterford, Ireland. I received this from a friend when my father died, and I found it very comforting. In trying to explain why they couldn't see granddaddy anymore, I also summarized it for my children:

Death is nothing at all — I have only slipped away into the next room. Whatever we were to each other, that we are still. Call me by my own familiar name. Speak to me in the easy way which you always used to. Laugh as we always laughed at the little jokes we enjoyed together. Play, smile, think of me, pray for me. Let my name be the household word that it always was. Let it be spoken without effort. Life means all that it ever meant, it is the same as it ever was, there is absolutely unbroken continuity. Why should I be out of your mind because I am out of your sight? I am but waiting for you, for an interval, somewhere very near — just around the corner. All is well. Nothing is past; nothing is lost. One brief moment and all will be as it was before — only better, infinitely happier and forever — we will all be one together again.

Although we want to protect our children from many of the horrors of the world, when something terrible is going on within the household, it is extremely difficult to protect them from the pain of what is happening right around them. Therefore, the best thing that we can do for them is to teach them tools to cope. It is important that you DO protect them from outsiders who feel that they are helping by telling the child too much. Inform those close to you how you want things to be handled with your children. However, sharing feelings with trusted individuals and asking for help is a valuable step in most healing processes. The following is a list of things to watch for in your child that may be signs that they are having emotional difficulties:

- having trouble concentrating
- crying easily
- eating more or less than usual
- poor grades in school or poor behavior reports from the teacher
- **silence** — it may seem normal, but it can sometimes be their only cry for help

In the book, *Becky and the Worry Cup*, by Wendy Harpham, she suggests giving your child a worry cup to place their worries in — rather than holding them inside. I have heard many versions of this, but whatever you choose, letting your child have an imaginary place to put their worries away can be very helpful — even with everyday life. Simply have them choose a container, and then get pennies, buttons or something plentiful and have them explain each worry as they place one of the chosen objects into the container. After they have gone to bed, always empty the container so that it can be fresh and ready for another session.

If the tragedy is of another nature, such as the loss of a home in a natural disaster, or having to leave your home abruptly for any other reason, the following may be of assistance:

- If you are getting ready to evacuate, choose one precious item for them to hold.
- Assure them that although things may seem scary, the most important thing is that you stay together as a family. Anything else can be replaced.
- If the worst happens, and there is no home to return to, tell them stories about the many homes that you lived in while growing up and how a "home" is where the family is…it doesn't matter where!

Young children may not be able to express grief or shock the same as an adult. Encourage them to draw, write or playact their feelings when you can. They require catharsis as much as any grown-up.

This is a small list, but a start. Another extremely valuable gift that we can bestow upon our children is the ability to always look forward. Despite loss, death or devastation, life continues to move ahead. Teach them that the "horizon is a wonderful place..." because we never know what is out there waiting for us. Just remember, the best thing that we can do for those who depend on us is to simply be there for them...in good times and in bad.

Even from a dark night, songs of beauty can be born.
- Maryanne Radmacher-Hershey

THE TRUE MAGIC OF MOTHER'S INTUITION

A Mother's Bond

Holding her close
Her heart touching mine
All I could think
Was, "Oh how divine."

No greater a love
Could there ever be
No stronger a bond
Than between she and me.

The feelings that flowed
From my heart, mind and soul
Enlightened my spirit
As we again became whole.

A mother and child
From conception are one
And together they stay
Until this life is done.

Though disjoined at birth
Their soul-flow connection
Remains through their lives
With the deepest affection.

Forever united
Rhythmic in heart
A child and its mother
Are never apart.

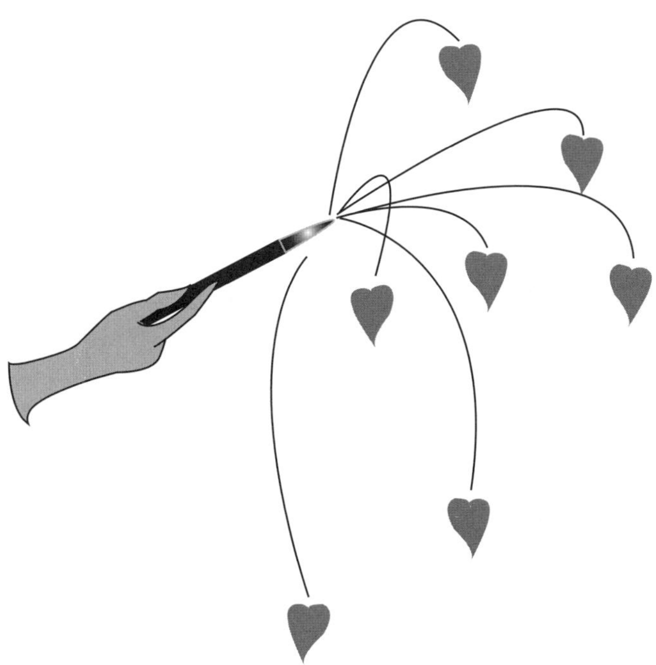

Maternal Telepathy— A Genuine Phenomenon

Have you ever reached for the phone to call your mother, only to have it ring...with her on the other end? Have you ever awakened in the middle of the night only seconds before your child cried out for you? Have you ever experienced the feeling that something was wrong with your child — and when you investigated found that you had arrived in the nick of time to stop the disaster? Has your child ever brought you something that you were just looking for?

For years I have had things like these happen, but hadn't researched the validity of it. In performing the research for this book however, I found that many studies had been performed in this area — with amazing stories and results. Some call it maternal instinct, which is easier for people to accept for some reason. I call it a gift from God, but call it what you may, it is a phenomenon that has occurred generation after generation after generation.

I wanted to end this book discussing this subject because I feel that it is the true magic that every mother can call upon from the depths of her soul. If you would like to enjoy a truly fascinating book on the subject, I would suggest the book, *A Mother's Link*, by Cassandra Eason. As a Fellow at the Alister Hardy Research Center for Religious Experience in Oxford, England, she has studied the subject thoroughly and offers a grand variety of compelling stories in her book.

When my own daughter Astra was only three years old, she proved to me that we indeed have a very special "link." One evening while we were on vacation in Southern California, we all sat watching a movie — pleasantly exhausted after a fun-filled day of swimming and sightseeing. I was sitting on the floor thinking of my mother and how much I missed her as I stared blankly at the movie. I thought I had done a superb job of hiding my sadness — and had not mentioned her at all that day. Out of the blue Astra walked over to me, cupped my face in her little hands and said, "Don't worry mommy, your mommy is okay." Tears filled my eyes and she hugged me as if she had become the mother and I the child. Whether she read my thoughts, or my mom had sent her a message to relate to me doesn't matter. Whatever the reason those precious words came out of her mouth, I was deeply thankful for the comfort that they brought.

In *A Mother's Link* there are many stories of how a mother saved her child's life by realizing that there was danger only seconds before it happened. One such story told by a mother in Salt Lake City, Utah goes as follows:

"...I felt an especially close bond with my second daughter Sarah and was told by family that we were too close. One evening when she was about eight months old I was in the kitchen and Sarah and her sister Monica were in the living room with my husband. Suddenly I had a terrible feeling. I rushed to the living room where my husband was reading and

Monica was playing. The baby was lying in the corner on her stomach apparently quite happy. I flipped her over and saw that she was silently choking on a balloon. My husband and Monica were not aware of the emergency."

In this extreme case, as well as thousands of others, it is obvious that mother's intuition is alive and well and living in every home where children dwell. The trick is to key into it in everyday levels of activity. I would sincerely like to encourage you to listen to your own heart when it concerns your own child. Only you know what is truly best for your children. All you have to do is be quiet and listen...the answers will come from within.

The Magic of a Mother's Intuition

By Suzan Schweizer

When I was about ten years old, my mother shocked me with her keen intuition. My brother Larry was returning home from Korea, and the whole family was anxiously awaiting his arrival. That morning my father headed down to the supply store where he often traded. As he entered the store, several of the men were obviously in a serious discussion. Seeing my father as he came through the door, one of the men said, "Did you hear? One of our planes that was returning to the States just went down. The reports say that a lot of our servicemen were aboard. Sad thing — they made it through the war and now...." My father stopped abruptly, as though he'd hit a brick wall. "LARRY!" That's all he could say before he collapsed.

The other men helped him up off the floor and brought him around. As soon as he recovered from the initial shock of hearing what had happened — and that it was the flight that his son was expected on, he called home. "Don't send Suzan to school. I'll be right home. I'll explain when I get there."

Of course my mom greeted him outside as he drove into the driveway. He gently explained the circumstances — and that Larry was listed as a passenger when suddenly Mother said, "Larry isn't on that plane! I can't tell you how I know, but he is NOT on that plane!" Five minutes after that LARRY CALLED. We rejoiced like we have never rejoiced before — or since. He had been trying to get through to us to let us know that he had indeed missed that plane and knew that we would be sick with worry. Little did he know that he HAD gotten through to our mother!

I could hardly believe my mother's telepathic ability at the time, but having been a mother now for over thirty years, I look back on the many times where I, too, have used this God-given capability. Maybe not in such dramatic illustrations, but certainly in situations where I have been needed. I can hardly count the times when I have called my own daughters and they've answered the phone with, "How do you always know when I need to talk with you?"

During the aftermath of the tragic earthquake in Turkey in August of 1999, I read an amazing story of a man who succeeded in finding his mother in the rubble after a dream he had about her. In the dream, his mother called to him saying, "Son, please help me. I'm here." He awakened knowing that his mother was alive — when everyone else had given up hope. He had already lost his son in the earthquake and his father had been hospitalized — so he was NOT going to give

cont.

up on finding his mother. The odds against finding her were worsened by the fact that she could not walk or talk, due to a stroke. As they dug through the ruins, the rescuers tried to convince him gently that there was little hope. He badgered them to keep searching. Then he heard a humming noise — the only noise his mother was able to make. It led him to his mother — and his dream came true.

Our sensitivity, our "mommy antennas," are up and quivering throughout our lifetime — for however we need to use them. It is indeed a gift to be cherished.

This is the only chapter where only one idea is offered. I simply suggest that you take at least five minutes a day to sit quietly and listen to that little voice that we all have inside of us. The answers and ideas that will come from the depths of your spirit will enlighten you — especially when you need them most. Listen to this guidance, follow it and trust it…and your journey through motherhood will be enhanced by an angel's care.

I think Dr. Benjamin Spock said it best…

What good mothers and fathers instinctively feel like doing for their babies, is usually best after all.

SEND US YOUR STORIES!

In completing this book, all I can say is…there is so much MORE I wanted to write! The point is that there are so many wonderful aspects of motherhood, and so MANY ways to enjoy and enhance the journey. My next project, however, is to include our fabulous partners…the DADDIES. Therefore, please send us any ideas and stories that you have concerning the magic that they perform in your children's lives to be included in:

DADDY MAGIC

— a book that will celebrate the joy of fatherhood and offer stories, ideas and suggestions to enhance the magic of a *father's* journey.

We're also gathering recipes for a future cookbook entitled:

COOKING UP SOME MAGIC

So send us your favorite recipe, along with a story about the fun of preparing it or the reason why it is special.

And remember, keep sending us your Mommy Magic stories as well, for the future:

MOMMY MAGIC II

We greatly value the input from our readers and look forward to hearing from you!

Please send all correspondence to:

Angel Power Press
P.O. Box 3327
Oceanside, CA 92051
or e-mail us at www.mommymagic.com

STORY CONTRIBUTORS

Val Acciani is a busy mother of two extremely active boys. After leaving a successful career in the retailing industry, she now works in the library of the school where her children attend...and loves it! She resides in San Diego with her husband, children, two cats and a guinea pig.

Tamara Amey is an ambitious and caring mom who shares her parenting skills and feelings with other mothers on the "Net." As manager of the ParentsPlace.com newsletter, she updates valuable information every week for its many subscribers who enjoy it.

Letitia Baldrige is America's best-selling author of books on manners, business conduct and human behavior. Her books have sold in the millions. She has had a distinguished career in government and business, having served in the American embassies in Paris and Rome and in the White House, as chief of staff to Jacqueline Kennedy. *Letitia Baldrige's More Than Manners: Raising Today's Kids to Have Kind Manners and Good Hearts,* is a really wonderful addition to every parent's library.

Sandi Bruegger lives in St. Louis, Missouri with her husband John and daughters, Madison and Skyler. She feels blessed to be a "stay-at-home" mom.

Ann Rogers Gallant was born and raised in Mobile, Alabama, and considers herself a true daughter of the South. After leaving her beloved Alabama to pursue a career in dance in Southern California, she returned home briefly to aid Vietnam War hero Jeremiah Denton in his successful campaign for the United States Senate. She then served for six years in the Senate in Washington, D.C. as a staff assistant to Senator Denton. She currently resides in Fairfax Station, Virginia with her husband Karl, and devotes her full time and energy to the magic of being a mother to sons Karl Jr. and Peirson.

Terry Lieberstein is the owner of Nature Watch, a company that provides innovative interactive nature programs for kids of all ages. She has a Master's Degree in Physical Geography and is also an accomplished folk singer and songwriter. Terry's CD entitled *Turkey Burps and T-Ball* is filled with fun, singable songs that are enjoyed by kids and adults alike. You can learn more about Terry and see the Nature Watch catalog on-line at http://naturific.com, or call 800-228-5816 for more information.

Jeanette Lisefski is the proud mother of three fantastic children and the founder of At-Home Mother Magazine and the National Association of At-Home Mothers. These resources provide mothers-at-home and those who want to be with a wide array of information, services, support and encouragement to help make at-home motherhood work for them. You can reach Jeanette at the National Association of At-Home Mothers, 406 E. Buchanan, Fairfield, IA 52556; fax her at 515-469-3068; or e-mail her at ahmrc@lisco.com. Be sure and check out the At-Home Website: AtHomeMothers.com.

Suzan Schweizer is the mother of three wonderful children, and is blessed with three terrific grandchildren.

Looking back at her child rearing days, she feels that her biggest accomplishment was in handling the difficulties of being a career Navy wife. Being creative, nurturing and loving her three children through thirteen relocations in twenty-five years has been her greatest challenge in life. She is an avid reader and traveler and loves to write in her spare time. She resides with her husband in Mission Viejo, California.

Lorena Serna is a happily married mother of a beautiful daughter. Being a military family, they travel extensively, but presently reside in Maryland. Designing Websites from home allows her the flexibility to move when necessary, as well as be near to her child.

Linda Sharp is a blissfully married mother of three adorable children and a big kid herself. Linda's observations on parenting have made folks laugh the world over! As an internationally published humorist, her articles appear weekly and monthly around the Web on the Internet and around the world in magazines. As creator and co-owner of SanityCentral.com, she offers a place for moms to go for a laugh. This Web site has won numerous awards and continues to be the chosen entertainment for those of us who rarely get out of the house! She is presently working on her first book, which will be a collection of the marvelous stories and anecdotes that have appeared on this site.

Linda O'Leary Sheetz is a highly respected instructor for "Redirecting Children's Behavior" seminars. She is the proud mother of two loving, sensitive and independent-thinking children.

ABOUT THE ARTIST

Daria Smith is a graphic designer/illustrator living on the Puget Sound in Bellingham, Wa. She counts herself among the very fortunate moms who have been able to find a way to combine a successful career along with the even more rewarding work of raising two beautiful and wonderful children...*she also admits her husband had something to do with it!* She can be reached by fax at (360) 734-8262.

BIBLIOGRAPHY

Eason, Cassandra. *The Mother Link*, Berkeley, CA: Seastone, 1999.

Linkletter, Arthur G. *Kids Still Say the Darndest Things*, New York: Bernard Geis Associates, 1959.

Shaw, Eva. *For the Love of Children*, Deerfield Beach, FL: Health Communications, 1998.

Internet Sources

Inspirational Quotes: The Collection

Good Quotations By Famous People

Famous Quotes

PERMISSIONS

"Forever, For Always and No Matter What." Reprinted with permission of Jeanette Lisefski. Copyright 1997 Jeanette Lisefski.

"Holding Grandma's Hand." Reprinted with permission of Tamara Amey and ParentsPlace.com.

SPREAD THE MAGIC

To order additional copies of *MOMMY MAGIC* for your friends and family, check your leading bookstore, or simply fill out the form below and send it along with your check to:

Angel Power Press, P.O. Box 3327, Oceanside, CA 92051

For faster service call us toll free at: 888-348-7563. Simply provide your credit card number and expiration date and we will ship your order immediately.

Also available is *TOUCHED BY A RAINBOW*, a delightful book of poems, also written by Adria Manary. Doreen Gentzler, news anchor for NBC, said the following about this unique collection: "Anyone who has ever held a new baby, lost a loved one, or simply paused to savor one of life's precious experiences, will find something meaningful here."

Please send me ____ copies of *MOMMY MAGIC* at $12.95 each and ____ copies of *TOUCHED BY A RAINBOW* at $11.95 each. Please add $2.00 per book for shipping. California residents please add sales tax.

My check or money order for $________ is enclosed.

OR please charge my MasterCard or Visa through the information below:

Name ____

Organization ______________________________________

Address ____

City / State / Zip ___________________________________

Card #______________________ Expiration Date ________

Signature ____

You can also fax your order to 760-721-6699, or order on the web by visiting www.mommymagic.com

Photo by Tom Glasco

About The Author

Adria Hilburn Manary is a writer, poet, public speaker and work-at-home mom. Although she has earned many titles in her successful career, her favorite title is "MOM." Pictured above with her husband Joel, their children — Chase, Astra and Dane, and their furry family members — Champagne and Casey...her home life is full! She is also the author of *Touched By A Rainbow*, co-author of *Kennedys — The Next Generation*, and creator of *The Washington Fun Times* newspaper.